Measuring and improving research impact

Crafting your career
in academia

Anne-Wil Harzing

Edition: May 2023

ISBN 978-1-7396097-5-7 (paperback, black & white)

Published by Tarma Software Research Ltd, UK

Author	Harzing, Anne-Wil
Title	Measuring and Improving Research Impact. Crafting your career in academia / Anne-Wil Harzing
Edition	1st ed.
ISBN	978-1-7396097-5-7 (paperback, black & white)
Subjects	Academic careers, academic publishing, academic development
Dewey Number	650.14

Table of contents

Introduction

When starting their career, many academics are mainly interested in getting their work published; see also my book *Publishing in academic journals* (2022). However, publishing your work should not be seen as the "end product" of doing research. If research funding can be seen as an "input" measure, publication is a "throughput" measure, with the ultimate purpose being impact. If our published work doesn't have impact, why publish?

This short book provides you with a lay introduction to measuring and improving research impact. Chapter 1 focuses on the *concepts*, discussing what research impact is, and how it differs by academic role. We will also delineate it from related concepts such as research quality and research evaluation.

Chapter 2 focuses on *measuring* research impact. It provides you with a crash course, discussing both traditional and new data sources and metrics. It also shows you how to establish your citation record with the free Publish or Perish software.

Subsequently, we move on from measuring impact to *presenting* and *evaluating* research impact. Chapter 3 demonstrates how to make your case for research impact, whereas Chapter 4 looks at the role of metrics versus peer review in evaluating research impact.

The next two chapters focus on *improving* your own research impact, discussing the four Cs of getting cited (in an ethical way!) in Chapter 5, and outlining a 7-step process to improve your research impact in Chapter 6.

Chapter 7 concludes this short book by emphasising the importance of impactful research *processes* that complement impactful research *outcomes*. It discusses the five key values of the HuMetrics initiative that should underlie an impactful research process: equity, openness, collegiality, soundness, and community.

I hope this short guide will help to demystify the topic of research impact in academia for you, and will provide you with the tools to be successful in creating your own research impact. I would love to hear from you if you feel this book has helped you; feel free to get in touch with me at anne@harzing.com.

Note: This short book is an edited and curated collection of my white papers, blogposts, and presentations on research impact, published between 2020 and 2023.

Chapter 1: What is impact?

In this first chapter, we look at what research impact is and discuss how it differs by academic role: research, teaching, and external engagement. Unfortunately, the concept is not unambiguous. When talking about research impact, academics have very different understandings of it. Worse still, they may not even be aware that different interpretations are possible.

As a result, any discussion about research impact soon descends in a Babylonian speech confusion. It also means that many academics are struggling to evidence research impact, for instance when making a case for promotion; see *Writing effective promotion applications* (2022). So, what is impact?

Defining impact

Oxford dictionary defines impact as "a marked effect or influence". Research impact means that our research has affected or influenced something or someone. Unfortunately, this immediately throws up even more questions:

- *Whom* has it impacted, i.e., who is the target audience?

- *How* has it made an impact, i.e., what was its ultimate goal?

- Through what *means* has this impact occurred, i.e., what are the primary outlets?

- How do we *know* this impact has occurred, i.e., how can we measure it?

The answer to these four questions depends on the specific academic role we are looking at (See the Table below). Academic jobs include three distinct roles: research, teaching, and external engagement, with each of these roles offering potential for research impact.

Research impact by academic role

Research impact differs by academic role and can be distinguished by audience, goal, outlet, and measures (see below). Our academic roles related to teaching and external engagement will also display impact that is unrelated to research. However, in this book we will focus on research impact only.

Academic Role	Whom? Target Audience	How? Ultimate goal	Through which means? Primary outlets	How do we know? Measures
Research	Other academics	Progress scientific knowledge	Academic journals, Research Monographs, Conferences	Citations in academic journals / books / conference papers
Teaching	Students	Develop critical thinking skills	Textbooks, Practitioner journals	Citations in textbooks / syllabi
External Engagement	Industry, Government, Public and society	Address societal problems	Practitioner journals / magazines, Policy reports, (Social) Media, Collaborative projects	Citations in policy documents, policy / legal changes, improved HDI / SDG

HDI = United Nations Human Development Index
SDG = United Nations Sustainable Development Goals

Research role

In the research role of our academic jobs, our target audience is other academics, and our ultimate goal is to progress scientific knowledge through the incorporation of our work in the broader scholarly body of knowledge.

We connect with our target audience – other academics – through academic journals, research monographs, and conferences. Preferred types of outlets, however, are highly dependent on disciplinary norms and preferences. In the Life Sciences and the Natural Sciences academic journals "rule". In the Humanities and some of the Social Sciences books are still a popular medium. In some Engineering disciplines, conference papers are a widely accepted way of diffusing knowledge quickly.

—

4

Whether or not we have influenced other academics is typically measured by citations in academic journals, books, and conference papers. Although we know that academics are sometimes careless in their referencing (See also my blogpost: *Are referencing errors undermining our scholarship and credibility?*), and there are many reasons to cite papers, we would normally expect citations to signify at least *some* level of impact on the work of the citing academic.

Citations can be field normalised to account for differences in citation practices across disciplines. We will discuss the different research metrics in much more detail in Chapter 2, where we also learn how to do citation analysis with Publish or Perish. In Chapter 5, I will show you how to increase the chances that your research is cited.

Teaching role

As academics, we can all have a tremendous impact on our students. Some of this impact will be unrelated to the research we do. In any good university, however, research is expected to feed into the classroom. Students benefit from research-informed teaching, allowing them to develop their critical thinking skills.

As academics, we facilitate this directly through prescribing our own and other academics' research as course readings. In many cases, though, we need to "translate" our research in order to make it more accessible for a student audience. We do so through publishing textbooks or articles in practitioner journals.

So, how do you know whether your research has diffused beyond your own classroom? First, you can find out whether your research is cited in textbooks by using Google Books. It might be difficult, however, to differentiate citations in textbooks from citations in monographs and practitioner books. Therefore, another option is to do a search in half a dozen key textbooks in your field.

To discover whether your publications (both your academic articles and textbooks or practitioner articles) are listed in teaching syllabi, Open Syllabus Explorer is an incredibly useful tool (See my blogpost *"Open Syllabus Explorer: evidencing research-based teaching?"*).

This option is particularly helpful if you have authored a textbook; obviously textbooks are much more likely to appear in syllabi than academic articles. For instance, using Open Syllabus I was able to show that my IHRM textbook appeared more than 500 time in syllabi (see screenshot below). To my considerable surprise, I discovered it was used not just in universities in the UK, North America, and Australia, but also in a variety of European countries, and in more than three dozen Indian universities. How cool is that?

Don't give up on your academic articles though. You might be pleasantly surprised! 36 of my academic articles appeared in syllabi. If you are junior, you are unlikely to see many of your articles featured in syllabi, but even if you find only *one* case that can still be argued to be indicative of future leadership in teaching.

Titles by all persons named: Anne Wil Harzing

	TITLES	APPEARANCES	SCORE
1	International Human Resource Management *Anne-Wil Harzing* SAGE, 1995	521	26
2	An Empirical Analysis and Extension of the Bartlett and Ghoshal Typology of Multinational Companies *Anne-Wil Harzing* Journal of International Business Studies, 2000	25	2
3	Are Our Referencing Errors Undermining Our Scholarship and Credibility? The Case of Expatriate Failure Rates *Anne-Wil Harzing* Journal of Organizational Behavior, 2002	24	2
4	The Relative Impact of Country of Origin and Universal Contingencies on Internationalization Strategies and Corporate Control in Multinational Enterprises: Worldwide and European Perspectives *Anne-Wil Harzing, Arndt Sorge* SAGE, 2003	20	1
5	Acquisitions Versus Greenfield Investments: International Strategy and Management of Entry Modes *Anne-Wil Harzing* Strategic Management Journal, 2002	20	1
6	Of Bears, Bumble-Bees, and Spiders: The Role of Expatriates in Controlling Foreign Subsidiaries *Anne-Wil Harzing* Elsevier, 2001	18	1

Engagement role

So far, we discussed the two key functions of *any* university: research and teaching. But there is also a third function: external engagement. This captures the impact our research has on industry, government, and the public/society at large, with the ultimate goal of addressing key societal problems. It is the kind of impact incorporated in Impact Case Studies in the UK Research Excellence Framework (REF), which is defined as *"an effect on, change or benefit to the economy, society, culture, public policy or services, health, the environment, or quality of life, beyond academia"*.

Making our research accessible to a non-academic audience typically requires "translating" it through writing up articles for practitioner-/professional journals and magazines, as well as publishing policy reports. It may also involve the use of (social) media, not just in order to diffuse our already published work, but also to allow continued engagement of non-academic audiences in our research. Integration of non-academic stakeholders from inception of research projects is increasingly common.

Overton is the world's largest searchable index of policy documents, guidelines, think tank publications and working papers.

Measuring this type of impact is quite challenging, however. Recent efforts like Overton (see above screenshot) might help. Academics might also be able to evidence changes in for instance government policy or legislation that are linked to their research. A more general case for impact could be made by referring to frameworks such as the United Nations Human Development Index or their Sustainable Development Goals.

Altmetrics are another frequently used source of evidence. They measure how often research is referenced in social media, online news media, online reference managers, and so on. However, it is important to realise that, rather than this being evidence of *impact*, it is more akin to a measure of attention. Whilst this may well create a "pathway to impact", Altmetrics cannot in and of themselves demonstrate actual societal impact.

Research impact: horses for courses

It is important to realise that different universities might have very different research impact strategies, especially with regard to their research and engagement roles. In the 2021 Research Excellence Framework (REF), the national research evaluation in the UK, the field of Business & Management showed a completely different ranking of universities depending on which of the composite criteria you focused on. This is evidenced by an analysis by the Chartered Association of Business Schools (see screenshots below).

Traditional research universities such as London Business School, the London School of Economics, and University College London excelled in the quality of their publications (see first screenshot), but only displayed an average performance in terms of societal impact. In contrast, Middlesex University, the University of Westminster – both modern universities – and SOAS (the School of Oriental and African Studies) topped the list for societal impact (see second screenshot below). However, they only had an average performance when looking at the quality of their publications. Only two universities score in the top 10 on both measures of research impact.

BUSINESS AND MANAGEMENT UOA 17 - OUTPUT 'POWER'

Outputs account for 60% of a provider's overall outcome (previously 65% for REF 2014) and are comprised of published or otherwise publicly available products of research in various forms.

Institution name	FTE of submitted staff	% of eligible staff submitted	4*	3*	2*	1*	Unclas-sified	Volume	GPA	GPA x volume	Output GPA Rank 2021
London Business School	106.45	100%	78.5	17	3.4	1.1	0	258	3.73	960.62	1
University of Cambridge	61.2	100%	71.1	23	5.2	0.7	0	148	3.65	539.84	2
The London School of Economics and Political Science	101.58	100%	68.4	25.7	5.1	0.8	0	246	3.62	889.14	3
Imperial College of Science, Technology and Medicine	92.15	100%	67.5	27.2	4.4	0.9	0	223	3.61	805.71	4
University College London	38.6	100%	61.9	32.9	5.2	0	0	93	3.57	333.20	5
The University of Warwick	158.15	100%	53.2	40	6.5	0.3	0	383	3.46	1324.60	6
The University of Bath	94.7	100%	50.9	39.9	9.2	0	0	229	3.42	783.09	7
City, University of London	124.55	85%	51.8	36.9	10.7	0.6	0	301	3.40	1024.50	8
University of Exeter	79.1	100%	50.6	38.8	10	0.6	0	191	3.39	649.69	9
The University of Surrey	53.55	100%	47.8	38.8	13.4	0	0	130	3.34	433.35	10

BUSINESS AND MANAGEMENT UOA 17 - IMPACT GPA

Impact accounts for 25% of a provider's overall outcome, up from 20% in REF 2014, and is based on impact case studies submitted by providers that demonstrate the impact of their research beyond academia, extending to the economy, society, culture, public policy or services, health, the environment or quality of life.

Institution name	FTE of submitted staff	% of eligible staff submitted	4*	3*	2*	1*	Unclas-sified	GPA	Impact Rank
Middlesex University	85.75	55	78.6	21.4	0	0	0	3.79	1
School of Oriental and African Studies	19.5	100	75	25	0	0	0	3.75	=2
The University of Westminster	47.35	25	75	25	0	0	0	3.75	=2
University of Exeter	79.1	100	71.4	28.6	0	0	0	3.71	4
The University of Manchester	163.1	100	75	20	5	0	0	3.70	5
University of Oxford	84.2	100	64.3	35.7	0	0	0	3.64	6
Cranfield University	40.1	100	62.5	37.5	0	0	0	3.63	7
The University of Leeds	144.53	100	61.1	38.9	0	0	0	3.61	=8
The University of Sheffield	139.85	100	61.1	38.9	0	0	0	3.61	=8
University of Glasgow	127.33	100	61.1	38.9	0	0	0	3.61	=8
City, University of London	124.55	85	66.7	27.7	5.6	0	0	3.61	=8

Research impact, quality, and reputation

In defining the construct of research impact, we also need to carefully distinguish it from other, related, constructs. This includes research quality and research reputation. Below, I have attempted to sketch these relationships, as well as the role of research communication in achieving both research impact and reputation.

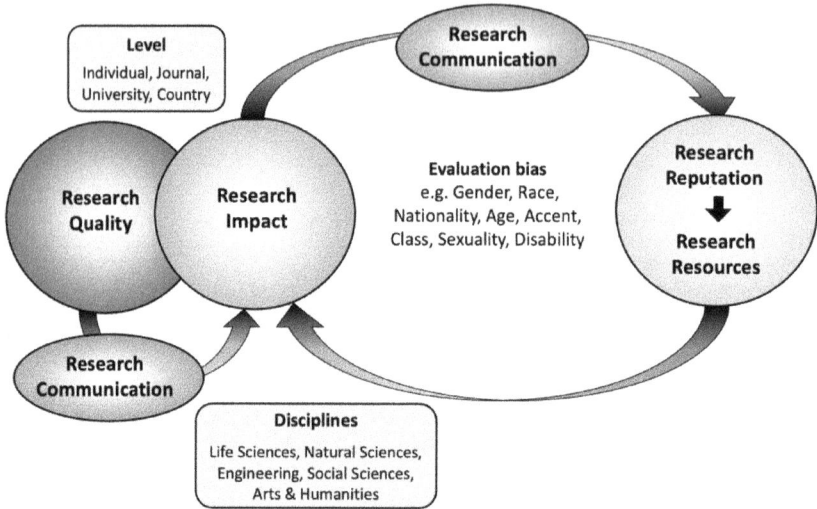

Research quality and research impact

Academic research impact – typically operationalised by citations – is often seen as a measure of research quality. Although by no means synonymous, the two concepts are undoubtedly related. In Chapter 5, where I discuss "the four C's of getting cited" I argue that competence (quality) is the first of the four C's.

Research quality is also a conditio-sine-qua-non. Without a certain minimum quality level, the three other C's (collaboration, care, and communication) will have little impact on citations. Of course, we can always find exceptions to this rule, but on average shoddy work will attract few citations and high-quality, meaningful work is more likely to be cited.

There are, however, elements of research quality that might *not* be captured by research impact. They are mainly related to the research *process* (see also Chapter 7) and include the rigour with which the research has been conducted, abstention from questionable research practices, and the extent to which Open Science practices have been followed. In addition, research quality should also incorporate the extent to which research cultures are inclusive of different perspectives and different demographics.

Research communication

Research communication is a very important facilitator – or when using academic terms: a mediator – to "translate" research quality into research impact. Remember though, it is a mediator only, it should not be an end in itself! Research communication can include presenting your work at conferences and research seminars (or webinars). Increasingly, however, it also includes engaging with social media, for instance through blogging about your work and sharing it on platforms such as ResearchGate, Twitter and LinkedIn. For more information on this see my book "*Creating social media profiles*" (2023).

Some academics might read your articles without you publicising them. This may happen through communications from academic journals and publishers as well as academics' own literature search strategies. However, with increasing publication outputs, a growing number of new journals, as well as more interdisciplinary research, these signals are much weaker than they were in the past. So, proper research communication is essential if you want your research to reach the right audience (academic or non-academic). We'll discuss this in more detail in Chapter 6.

Research reputation and evaluation bias

Combining research quality and research impact with research communication is likely to create a strong research reputation. Although in this book my emphasis is on individual academics, this relationship also holds for journals, universities, and countries. However, as shown in the above figure, the strength of the relationship and the exact operationalisation of the various concepts might vary for these different levels of analysis and different disciplines.

Unfortunately, at the heart of the whole process also lies a distortion to the "objective" measurement of the various concepts. Every single variable and relationship in the model can be subject to bias. First, the same research quality is often evaluated differently depending on the academic's demographics.

Second, the extent to which research quality leads to citations to your work is subject to these same biases, as is the extent to which research communication leads to reputation building. Even the relationship between research reputation and research resources is fraught with bias.

Most of my own experience and advocacy has been around gender bias, where the Matilda effect (a bias against acknowledging the achievements of women scientists whose work is attributed to their male colleagues) is well-established. However, there are also strong negative effects in other areas listed in the figure (race, nationality, age, accent, class, sexuality, disability).

In sum

In this first chapter, we defined what research impact is and how it differs by academic role, looking at the audience, goal, outlets, and measurement. We also delineated it from related concepts such as research quality and research reputation. In the remainder of this book, we will focus mainly on the research role of our academic jobs. First, in Chapter 2, we will look at the data sources and metrics that can be used to measure academic research impact.

Chapter 2: Getting savvy about data sources and metrics

In Chapter 1, I showed that academic research impact – i.e., research impact related to the research role of our academic job – is typically evaluated by citation metrics. But where can you find these citations, what are these other metrics that you hear about such as the journal impact factor and the h-index, and how do you calculate them?

This chapter will take you on a crash course about data sources and metrics for citation analysis, discussing the Web of Science, Scopus, Google Scholar, and newer data sources, as well as the traditional and newer research metrics. It closes by showing you how to calculate these metrics with the free Publish or Perish software.

Data sources

Until the mid 1990s, the Web of Science (WoS) had a monopoly on citation data. But since then, the landscape has become increasingly varied. Scopus and Google Scholar are the two key alternatives, but in the last 5 years at least half a dozen new contenders have sprung up. We will discuss each of the key alternatives in turn.

Web of Science: a focus on the Sciences

When I started writing my Master's thesis in the 1980s, the analysis of citations was synonymous with the Web of Science, which offered a product called the Science Citation index. Launched in 1964 it was originally produced by the Institute for Scientific Information and created by Eugene Garfield. In the early days of my academic career – and remember that I started my career when the world wide web didn't exist yet and email was still in its infancy – it consisted of heavy volumes of books with wafer-thin, almost see-through, paper.

To find out which articles had cited the article you were interested in, you would go to the library and carry these back-breaking books to a table to laboriously track down all its citing articles. Given the inevitable delays in producing these volumes, any citation analysis would effectively miss the most recent years of citations. Even so, the Science Citation Index was quite revolutionary when it was first launched. It was a way to understand how a field of research had developed from its seminal articles. Before the introduction of the Science Citation Index, all you could do was look at the references in an article, but that was looking *backward*, not *forward*.

Fast forward thirty years and now citations are not just used to do literature research, but also to evaluate academics. We might well feel this is not a positive development, I have certainly voiced my concerns about this (see e.g., "*When knowledge wins: transcending the sense and nonsense of academic rankings*"). But this is not something you or I can change overnight, so that is not what this chapter is about. However, it does mean that any decisions about data sources and metrics impact on individual academics' careers.

Like many scientific developments, the Web of Science started out in the Natural Sciences and Life Sciences. As a result, the articles and journals covered in the Web of Science tend to be mostly journals in these two disciplines. They also tend to be international journals in the English language. The Web of Science has introduced a Social Sciences Citation Index as well as an Arts and Humanities index in the 1970s. Even so, coverage in these disciplines always remained much lower than in the Natural Sciences and Life Sciences, with the Engineering discipline falling in between. Whereas more than 90% of the journals in Microbiology are covered in the Web of Science, this might be as low as 20% in some of the Arts and Humanities.

This lack of substantive coverage outside the Sciences – combined with its *very* hefty price tag – is the biggest drawback of the Web of Science. In this short guide, I lack the space to discuss its other flaws. However, if you are interested in exploring these, refer to chapter 4 of my book *Using the Publish or Perish Software* (2023).

Scopus and Google Scholar: broader coverage

After 30 years of a Web of Science monopoly, Elsevier introduced Scopus in 1996. Scopus provided a more comprehensive coverage of publications than the Web of Science, especially for Engineering and the Social Sciences. Both Scopus and the Web of Science, however, primarily focused on journal publications. They also covered mainly English language journals, the traditional outlet for the Natural and Life Sciences. In contrast, conference papers are both important and prestigious outlets in the Engineering disciplines. Moreover, for the Social Sciences and Humanities books, book chapters, publications in local and regional journals – including publications in languages other than English – are important. Like the Web of Science before it, Scopus struggled to incorporate these "non-traditional" publication outlets to any significant extent.

The introduction of Google Scholar in 2004 therefore was a major step forward as it covered *any* publication that Google was able to parse from websites they identified as publishing academic content. This included not just articles in English-language journals, but also publications in other languages, conference papers, research reports, working papers, and even data and software. And yes, I am aware that several of these publications might not be considered "proper" academic work, certainly not in all fields. But remember that for our current purposes we are not looking for accurate *publication* counts, we are looking for evidence of research impact, i.e., citations. Non-academic publications will typically not be highly cited. And if they are, they clearly have an impact on the field, so they deserve to be counted!

As Google Scholar covers a far wider range of publication types, it will report a much larger number of publications and citations for disciplines in which publications other than journal articles are commonplace. The graph below showed the results of a study in which I compared citation levels in the Web of Science and Google Scholar for 20 Nobel prize winners in four distinct disciplines: Chemistry, Economics, Medicine, and Physics. Whereas for the Life and Natural Sciences citation levels were relatively similar in these two data sources, for Economics they varied dramatically, being nearly seven times as high in Google Scholar as in the Web of Science.

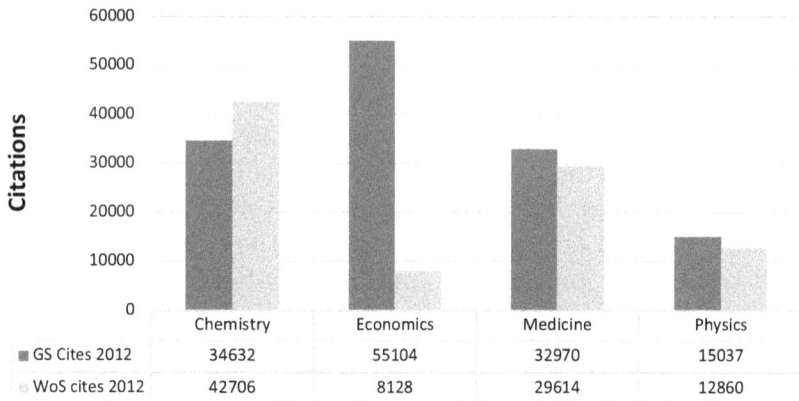

Citations	Chemistry	Economics	Medicine	Physics
GS Cites 2012	34632	55104	32970	15037
WoS cites 2012	42706	8128	29614	12860

Even though the five Nobel Prize winners in Economics on average had the lowest number of citations in the Web of Science, they had by far the *highest* number of citations in Googles Scholar. This reversal occurred because many of their most impactful – and most highly cited – publications were books, rather than journal articles. This is a pattern that is very common in the Social Sciences more generally, with academics in the Social Sciences on average having 3-6 times as many citations in Google Scholar than in the Web of Science. Any comparison of publication and citation counts between disciplines will therefore vary dramatically depending on the data source used.

New kids on the block

Since the mid 2010s, many new data sources have been launched, including the Lens, Microsoft Academic, Semantic Scholar, CrossRef, Dimensions, and most recently Open Alex. In the past years, I have conducted bibliometric research investigating comparative coverage in Microsoft Academic, CrossRef and Dimensions, and I will do the same for Semantic Scholar and Open Alex soon. My free citation analysis software Publish or Perish, discussed in the last section of this chapter, also allows you to easily compare coverage for many of these data sources.

My research showed that Microsoft Academic presented an excellent compromise between coverage and data quality. In coverage it was very close to Google Scholar for journal publications, and it had a very decent coverage of non-journal publications. At the same time, it presented a much cleaner set of data than Google Scholar. Unfortunately, Microsoft has discontinued Microsoft Academic in January 2022, although Open Alex aims to provide a replacement for it. My research also showed that CrossRef and Dimensions presented good alternatives to Scopus and the Web of Science, but still lagged quite far behind Google Scholar in terms of coverage.

Traditional metrics

Metrics are quantitative measures designed to help evaluate research outputs. They generally come in two forms: metrics that are based on publication and citation counts, and Altmetrics. This section will focus on the former, discussing the traditional metrics (publications, citations, and the journal impact factor) as well as the newer h-index metric and its variants.

We briefly discussed Altmetrics in the context of societal impact. They measure how often research is referenced in e.g., social media, online news media, and online reference managers. It is important to note though that, rather than this being evidence of *impact*, it is more akin to a measure of attention. For more information on the source of these Altmetrics, see my book *Creating Social Media Profiles* (2023).

Publications

Publication metrics count the number of academic publications such as articles, books, book chapters, and conference papers. Using this metric to evaluate research is problematic for two reasons. First, simply counting publications ignores the quality differences *between* publications. Depending on the level of the conference and the discipline, a conference paper might take a few days to write, a serious research monograph might well take a year or even several years.

But even within the same category, such as journal publications, there are vast quality differences. A publication in a low-level journal with un-demanding peer review might only take a few weeks to write and a few months to get published. In contrast, publications in the top journals in my own field – Business & Management – might take many months to write and polish, and one to three years to get through several rounds of very demanding peer review.

The second problem is that a publication metric is heavily dependent on publication practices within a discipline. In the Life Sciences and some of the Natural Sciences high performing academics might well publish several articles every month. But these articles are short and might be the product of lab research in which individuals only have a minor input in every paper. In these fields, it is not unusual for publications to have dozens – or in some case even hundreds – of co-authors, with only one or two of them playing a significant role in writing up the paper. The review process is generally quite quick with manuscripts often published within months of submission.

In the Humanities, academics might be working for many years on a single book. In the Social Sciences co-authorships are more common, but they rarely exceed five, with two or three authors being most common. Papers are often 20-40 pages long and go through three or four rounds of revisions with five to ten pages of reviewer comments not unusual for some journals. They can take many years to publish. Hence, in most of the Humanities and Social Sciences academics would be very happy to publish one or two good papers a year.

These differences play out at the institutional level too. When I was Research Dean, I once had a fraught discussion with my Deputy Vice Chancellor Research – a medical academic – about the performance of our Faculty of Economics & Business which he saw as "mediocre". He argued that we should double or even triple our output. Showing him data from the Web of Science Essential Science Indicators and several university rankings, I finally managed to convince him that we already ranked in the top-30 in Economics & Business world-wide. Even doubling our performance would see us shooting up to #1, leaving Harvard, Stanford, and MIT a very long way behind us. Comparisons across disciplines are always fraught whatever the level of analysis.

Citations

After publications, the number of citations to an academic's body of work is probably the second most used research metric. As briefly highlighted in the previous section, and discussed in more detail in Chapter 4, the number of recorded citations can differ dramatically between data sources. However, even when using a comprehensive data source – such as Google Scholar – disciplinary differences in the number of citations are not "erased" entirely.

Beyond disciplinary differences, there are three additional problems in using citations as a measurement of research impact. First, just like publications, citations can differ in "quality". Second, in many of the disciplines – and especially in the Social Sciences and Humanities – publications only start gathering citations after a few years. Third, citations can be very skewed. This is true not only at the level of universities and journals, but also for an individual academic's record.

Citation "quality": not all citations are alike

Some citations are very superficial and only refer to someone's work in a tokenistic way; other citations engage deeply with a publication. Yet other publications might be *refuting* the work they are referring to. For those categorically opposed to metrics, the latter is often used as an argument against the use of citations, although as we will see below refuting – also called contrasting – citations are very rare.

In recent years, services have sprung up that try to "rate" citations. Scite_ for instance divides citations into three categories: supporting, mentioning, and contrasting, based on "*rhetorical function*". Semantic Scholar identifies highly influential citations (see screenshot below; the lightbulb indicates influential citations), based on "*a number of factors including the number of citations to a publication, and the surrounding context for each*". These services clearly have a lot of potential. However, their classification methods are not yet very transparent. Moreover, the percentage of citations in the "default" category – i.e., mentioning or not being highly influential – typically lies between 94% and 98% of total citations, indicating low discriminatory power.

A review of two dozen academics in the Social Sciences showed these proportions do not differ much between academics in the same field. Semantic Scholar's highly influential citations were generally in the range of 5-6% of an academic's total citations. In the same discipline, Scite_'s supporting citations are typically in the 1.5-2.5% range and contrasting citations in the 0.1-0.3% range (see below). Although these services might thus be useful for doing literature reviews, they do not seem to add much value beyond "raw citations" in terms of measuring research impact. Moreover, their web services are often excruciatingly slow, making repeated searches very frustrating.

Citations are slow to pick up

In most disciplines citations only start picking up after a few years. This is especially true for the Social Sciences and Humanities, where the publication process is more drawn-out with multiple rounds of revisions. Accepted publications can also take a long time to appear in print. Thus, if someone is writing a paper in 2019 and cites a paper published in 2018, it might well take until 2022, 2023 or even 2024 before the citing paper appears in print. This means that in these fields it is hard to evidence impact for recently published papers.

In contrast, in disciplines such as Molecular Biology & Genetics or Astrophysics the time lapse between research and publication and publication and citation is generally much shorter. Papers are often published within a year of writing. Thus, citations to another paper will be visible within a year too. Hence, a PhD student or postdoc in these fields can be expected to have citations, but this is not usually true in the Social Sciences and Humanities.

As a corollary, citations obviously increase over time. This means comparing raw citations for academics at different career stages is inadvisable. The next section discusses some newer h-index based metrics that correct for career stage. However, simple metrics such as citations per year and annual citation counts can also help (see the last section of this chapter "Citation analysis in Publish or Perish"). Time-adjusted metrics like this provide a fairer comparison between academics with different lengths of publication history.

Citations might be highly skewed

Citations are highly skewed. This is true at the level of institutions, or departments, in that – depending on the size of the grouping – it is often a small group of highly-cited academics that account for most of the institution's citations. This is also true at the journal level. Some studies found a mere 15% of the articles to make up 50% of the citations in a journal and the most cited 50% of the articles to be cited, on average, ten times as often as the least cited half. The actual percentages will differ across journals, time, and disciplines, but the general principle still holds. In fact, the discovery of the general law of skewness in *any* bibliometric measure is one of the fundamental laws of bibliometrics. It is called Lotka's law (1926) after its author.

However, skewness can also occur within an individual academic's record. A high citation count might be due to one or a few papers, even papers that an individual has only been tangentially involved in as one of many authors. This is a particularly significant issue in the Life Sciences, where for instance guidelines for doing research in a specific area typically become very highly cited. One of my Life Science colleagues was one of over 2,000 academics to co-author guidelines for research on autophagy. The article's more than 11,000 citations to date make up more than 90% of her citation count.

However, this might also occur in the Social Sciences with articles that are particularly timely. Another one of my Middlesex colleagues was one of more than 40 academics co-authoring a timely article on using social and behavioural science to support COVID-19 research. Despite having been published recently, the article has nearly 5,000 citations and makes up well over half of his citation record.

Although no doubt both articles are of considerable significance, the non-lead authors in these articles have only made a very small contribution to them. As such these academics' citation count should be seen in a different light from those of academics who have achieved the same citation counts with articles that they single-authored, lead authored, or co-authored with a small group of colleagues. If you are using raw citations as a metric, it is therefore important to have a look at co-authorship patterns. Although this is hard to automate, even a quick glance at someone's publication record in Publish or Perish (see the section "Citation analysis in Publish or Perish") will easily identify these outliers, as well as other authorship patterns, such as the extent of single-authorship and lead authorship.

Journal impact factor (JIF)

After publications and citations, the JIF is probably the best-known research metric. It reflects the yearly mean number of citations in a particular year to the articles published in the last two years in a given journal. It is based on Clarivate's Web of Science data, though in 2016 Elsevier introduced a very similar metric, CiteScore, based on Scopus data. Launched in 1975, the JIF is the oldest "composite" research metric, i.e., a metric based on a *combination* of publications and citations, and is still firmly entrenched in many academic circles.

Its attraction might lie in the fact that it addresses *some* of the drawbacks of raw publications and citations. The JIF is seen as providing a "quality metric" for journals, thus addressing the issue of quality differences for publications. The higher the JIF, the higher the journal quality, and the quality of the articles in it. It also addresses the problem of the lack of citations to recent papers as the JIF can be used to estimate future citations for recently published papers by looking at the mean citation score for articles published in the journal.

Unfortunately, the JIF doesn't address disciplinary differences in publication and citation patterns. It also has a whole range of technical problems and has been shown to be open to manipulation by unscrupulous editors. Moreover, as we have seen above, citations within journals are heavily skewed. Hence, any metric based on mean citations may have very little value. As such, the number of articles pointing out the problems in using the JIF metric increased rapidly over the years; the last 5 years showed more than 200 articles with journal impact factor in the title.

However, the JIF's most significant drawback lies in its predominant usage, which reflects a conflation of levels of analysis. The JIF is a *journal* level metric, but JIFs are often used to evaluate individual *articles* published in the journal. As discussed above, citations are highly skewed. Not every publication in a journal with a high JIF will be highly cited, some publications published in journals with a low JIF have a lot of citations. Hence, using the JIF to evaluate individual articles – let alone individual academics – is ill-advised.

Newer metrics

Until the mid-2000s, publications, citations, and the JIF were the only metrics known in the wider academic community. Researchers in bibliometrics and scientometrics have long advocated more sophisticated measures, but these metrics never reached a wider audience. This changed with the publication of the h-index by physicist Jorge Hirsch in 2005, an index combining publications and citations. It took the academic world by storm, largely because it appears to have struck the right balance between sophistication and simplicity.

As a sign of its wide acceptance, it is prominently displayed in nearly all databases, including the Web of Science, Scopus, and Google Scholar. Just like for the JIF, there is a cottage industry of publications listing its drawbacks, but most of these relate to the two metrics it is composed of (publications and citations). Some of these drawbacks, e.g., its inability to compare across career stages and disciplines, have been (partially) resolved by the h-index variants discussed below.

h-index

The h-index is a statistic that tries to capture both publications and citations in one metric, but addresses some of the disadvantages of relying on *one* of these metrics only. It is defined as follows:

> *A scientist has index h if h of his/her Np papers have at least h citations each, and the other (Np-h) papers have no more than h citations each.*

If you have a h-index of 10 this means that you have 10 papers with at least 10 citations each. The h-index can run from 0 if you have no citations at all to over 100. However, most fields will have relatively few academics with h-indices over 40. The h-index thus combines an assessment of quantity (the number of publications) with an approximation of quality (impact, or citations to these papers).

An academic cannot have a high h-index without publishing a substantial number of papers. However, this is not enough, the papers need to be cited to be incorporated in the h-index. The h-index is therefore preferable over the number of papers, which might be boosted by writing many low-level papers. Unless these papers are impactful and highly cited, they will not count for the h-index. Hence the h-index favours academics that publish a continuous stream of papers with lasting and above-average impact.

The h-index is *also* preferably over the total number of citations as it corrects for "one hit wonders", i.e., academics who have authored (or co-authored) one or a limited number of highly cited papers but have not shown a sustained academic performance. As such the h-index addresses two key problems identified in our discussion of publications and citations: low-level publications and the very skewed nature of citations for some academics. However, it does not address incomparability across disciplines and career stages.

Moreover, the h-index cannot decrease over time. Even if academics never publish another paper or get another citation, their h-index will remain the same. This is also true for publications and citations, but this concern was only voiced frequently after the introduction of the h-index. In fact, many of the concerns against the h-index appear to be concerns against the use of metrics as such (see also Chapter 4).

---

h-index alternatives

The popularity of the h-index led to a barrage of attempts to improve on this metric, with well over fifty h-index variants or alternatives proposed to date. In my view, most of these attempts are missing the point of the h-index as a "sophisticated, but simple metric". Many variants try making the h-index more "accurate" or incorporate more of the academic's citations.

Attempting to make the h-index more "accurate" by calculating it with one or more decimal points, only creates an illusion of precision that is not warranted by the underlying metrics. Devising metrics that incorporate "excess citations" over and beyond those needed for inclusion in the h-index is an equally futile endeavour. If you are interested in citations, use citations as a metric. Metrics addressing the fact that the h-index doesn't include all papers or citations negate the very purpose of the h-index.

However, there are a few h-index alternatives attempting to address the two core problems of the h-index: its inability to compare across disciplines and its inability to compare across time and career stages.

hI,norm

The hI,norm, is an individual h-index which corrects for disciplinary differences in publication and citation patterns. One of the most important reasons for higher (lower) publication and citation levels is a larger (smaller) number of co-authors. A larger number of co-authors means each individual author needs to spend less time on a paper and can thus publish more papers. For reasons discussed in more detail in Chapter 5, a larger number of co-authors also leads to a larger number of citations.

Therefore, individual h-indices adjust the h-index for the number of co-authors, acknowledging the larger authorship contributions in the Humanities, Social Sciences and Engineering when compared to the Natural and Life Sciences. This follows a similar principle to the calculation of single-author equivalent publications where the number of publications is divided by the number of co-authors.

The first individual h-index was proposed by Batista *et al.* in a *Scientometrics* article in 2006, shortly after the original h-index. It divides the standard h-index by the *average* number of authors in the articles that contribute to the h-index; the resulting index is called hI. In the Publish or Perish software we have implemented a different individual h-index, the hI,norm, that takes a different approach: instead of dividing the total h-index by the number of co-authors, the hI,norm first normalizes the number of citations for each paper by dividing the number of citations by the number of authors for that paper. Then it calculates hI,norm as the h-index of the *normalised* citation counts. This approach is much more fine-grained; we believe that it more accurately accounts for any co-authorship effects that might be present. It is a better approximation of the per-author impact, which is what the original h-index set out to provide. We have kept the hI available in the PoP software for continuity purposes, but it is no longer shown as one of the key metrics.

Note that someone who co-publishes with others will not need to *publish* more articles to achieve the same hI,norm as an academic who publishes single-authored articles. However, the co-authored articles will need to gather more *citations* to become part of the hI,norm, as the article's citations will be divided by the number of co-authors. The example below, created in 2015, shows that academics with the same or very similar h-indices can have very different individual h-indices and visa versa.

h-index:	45	h-index:	44	h-index:	23	h-index:	18
g-index:	97	g-index:	79	g-index:	67	g-index:	53
hI,norm:	37	hI,norm:	20	hI,norm:	20	hI,norm:	18
hI,annual:	1.85	hI,annual:	0.91	hI,annual:	0.67	hI,annual:	0.45

The first box shows my own metrics in 2015. I am an academic in the Social Sciences with a substantial number of single-authored articles. The second screenshot presents a Physics Professor at the University of Melbourne with a similar h-index, but a much lower hI,norm. Most of his articles were co-authored with at least three other academics. The third and fourth screenshot show two other Professors at the same University (in the Social Sciences and Humanities) with a similar hI,norm as the Physics Professor, but with much lower h-indices. Their work was largely (or solely) single-authored.

26

hA-index

The hA-index is a relatively recent index and was proposed by Yves Fassin in the ISSI Newsletter in 2020. The calculation of the hA-index follows a similar pattern as the h-index, but divides the citation count of each paper by the age of the paper before ranking them and calculating the index as follows:

the h_a-index of a given dataset is the largest number of papers in the dataset that have obtained at least h_a citations per year on average.

In doing so, the hA-index gives a measure of the *sustained* citation *rate* of the data set, rather than only the total number of citations. This means that the hA-index provides a fairer comparison for academics at different career stages. Older academics will see their hA-index decline if their papers do not continue to accumulate citations at the same rate. Younger academics will see recent papers with a decent yearly citation rate, but a relatively low number of total citations, duly recognised in the hA-index.

hI,annual

The hI,annual (hIa for short), published by Harzing, Alakangas and Adams in 2014, was designed to address the two key problems of the h-index: its inability to compare academics in different disciplines and at different career stages. It is calculated by dividing the hI,norm, discussed above, by an individual's academic age, i.e., the number of years elapsed since their first publication

The hIa-index thus measures the average number of single-author equivalent h-index points that an academic has accumulated in each year of their academic career. A hIa of 1.0 means that an academic has consistently published one article per year that, when corrected for the number of co-authors, has accumulated enough citations to be included in the h-index. The last three last academics in the hI,norm example we discussed above have very different hI,annual indices (0.45-0.91), despite having similar hI,norm indices (18-20). This is because their academic age runs from 22 to 40 years.

To show how the hIa develops over different career stages, I have reproduced the metrics of four high-performing individuals at very different career stages. They have been publishing for 9, 20, 29, and 40 years respectively. As is immediately obvious, the h and hI,norm indices for these four academics differ very substantially. However, their hI,annual indices are very similar indeed. Using the hIa might thus be useful to "spot" high performers early in their career.

9 years		20 years		29 years		40 years	
h-index:	24	h-index:	45	h-index:	69	h-index:	82
g-index:	49	g-index:	97	g-index:	167	g-index:	212
hI,norm:	17	hI,norm:	37	hI,norm:	53	hI,norm:	69
hI,annual:	1.89	hI,annual:	1.85	hI,annual:	1.83	hI,annual:	1.73

Obviously, there is no guarantee that the younger academics will continue to grow their h-index (and thus hI,norm) over the next 10, 20 or 30 years. Unless academics keep publishing high-impact work and their current publications continue to acquire more citations, their hIa will decline naturally with age. Hence, maintaining a high hIa for more than 20 years is indicative of academics who are both very productive and impactful.

g-index

Although I do not believe that attempts to capture "excess citations" beyond the h-index are conceptually or practically very useful, there is one index, the g-index, that has received a considerable amount of attention. Hence, by popular demand it is included in the key metrics set in Publish or Perish (see next section). It is like the h-index in that it combines publications and citations, but it is weighed a bit more heavily towards citations. The g-index is calculated based on the distribution of citations received by a given researcher's publications, such that:

given a set of articles ranked in decreasing order of the number of citations that they received, the g-index is the unique largest number such that the top g articles received together at least g2 citations.

A g-index of 20 means that an academic has published at least 20 articles that *combined* have received at least 400 citations. However, unlike the h-index these citations *could* be generated by only a small number of articles. For instance, an academic with 20 papers, 15 of which have no citations with the remaining five having respectively 350, 35, 10, 3 and 2 citations would have a g-index of 20, but a h-index of 3 (three papers with at least three citations each).

Roughly, *h* is the number of papers of a certain "quality" [citations] threshold, a threshold that rises as h rises; *g* allows citations from higher-cited papers to be used to bolster lower-cited papers in meeting this threshold. Therefore, in all cases g is at least h, and is in most cases higher. However, unlike the h-index, the g-index "saturates" whenever the average number of citations for all published papers exceeds the total number of published papers; the way it is defined, the g-index is not adapted to this situation.

By definition, the maximum level of an academic's h-index and g-index is limited by the number of their papers. However, whereas in the case of the h-index this is not a *practical* limitation as papers still need to be cited to be included in the h-index; it is in the case of the g-index. This leads to the counterintuitive result that, once saturated, the g-index – a citation-based metric – will increase when publishing an additional paper, even if this paper never gets cited.

Citation analysis in Publish or Perish

In the previous sections, I reviewed three different data sources and eight different metrics. But how do you get access to these data sources? And how do you calculate these metrics? That is where the free Publish or Perish comes in, a software program that provides an interface to a variety of data sources. Please note that the name of the software is meant *ironically*, and was chosen for immediate name recognition among academics. It certainly doesn't mean that I support a Publish or Perish culture! The slide below, taken from one of my presentations on research impact, summarises the software's key features.

Your citation record in 7-8 data sources

- Publish or Perish software
  - Free, available since 2006
  - Used by > 1 million academics in 150+ countries
  - Increasing use by students
  - Windows & Mac
- Many use cases
  - Citation analysis
  - Literature reviews
  - Bibliometric research

Version 8: November 2021

Middlesex University London

For details see: The changing usage of Publish or Perish over the years: where, why, when, what & who?

For detail about Publish or Perish and its dozens of use cases refer to the training materials on my website, my many blogposts on the topic, as well as my forthcoming book: *Using the Publish or Perish software* (2023). Here I only present you with a few basics.

PoP provides an interface to a range of data sources. This currently includes Crossref, Google Scholar, Google Scholar Profiles, Pudmed, OpenAlex, Scopus, Semantic Scholar, and the Web of Science (only for users whose university has a subscription). However, by far the most popular data source is Google Scholar, mainly because of its more extensive coverage. The easiest way to get an overview of your metrics is with a Google Scholar profile search. If you do not have a Google Scholar profile, create one. If you don't know how to do this, refer to one of my blogposts (see Further reading at the end of this book) or my book *Creating social media profiles* (2023).

If you are looking for someone else's metrics and they don't have a Google Scholar profile, you can use a regular Google Scholar search. However, author disambiguation – finding only the publications of the author you are interested in and not those of their namesakes – can be hard, especially if the author has a common name. For tips on how to do this, refer to the PoP training materials or the *Using the Publish or Perish software* book.

Basic metrics

Publish or Perish provides access to all the metrics I discussed above, apart from the journal impact factor, which is copyrighted by Clarivate. The screenshot below shows my own metrics for August 2022, based on my Google Scholar Profile. The left-hand side displays basic metrics, such as the number of years that an academic has been publishing, their total number of publications and citations (which happened the be a nice round number on the day I took this screenshot). It also shows the average number of citations per year and per paper, as well as the average number of authors per paper.

Citation metrics	?		
Publication years:	1995-2022	h-index:	69
Citation years:	27 (1995-2022)	g-index:	154
Papers:	178	hI,norm:	55
Citations:	24000	hI,annual:	2.04
Cites/year:	888.89	hA-index:	25
Cites/paper:	134.83	Papers with ACC ≥ 1,2,5,10,20:	
Authors/paper:	2.02	125,109,80,60,30	

It is important, however, to realise the limitations of metrics using averages. Although my average number of citations per year is around 900, this varies from 100-200 per year in the early 2000s to closer to 2,000 per year since 2015. Likewise, the average number of citations per paper of nearly 135 includes sixteen publications with more than 500 citations and three with more than 1,000 citations, but also some 20 publications without any citations. Most of the latter are recent publications, conference papers or book reviews.

My authors/paper metrics shows that *on average* I published with only one co-author. However, my academic record is a combination of mostly single-authored publications in the early phases of my academic career, publications with one co-author in the middle phase of my career and publications with two and very occasionally three co-authors in more recent years. So, it is always important to look behind the averages and to compare different career stages for the same academic.

Composite metrics

The right-hand side of the screenshot above shows all the metrics we have discussed in some detail in the previous section. My h-index is 69; this means that I have published 69 articles that have at least 69 citations each. In a publication set comprised of 178 publications, ranging from publications in top journals and research monographs to book reviews, short conference papers and some blogposts, the h-index provides a useful first cut assessment of the number of *impactful* publications.

My g-index is 154; this means I have published 154 articles that combined have at least 23,716 citations. Like the h-index, this metric does incorporate publications as well as citations. However, in practice it is very highly correlated with the total number of citations. For academics with a substantial number of publications and an average number of cites/per paper that doesn't exceed the number of papers, the g-index is simply the square root of the number of citations. Hence, in many cases the g-index provides very little information over and beyond the number of publications and citations.

The next three metrics show the various h-index alternatives that correct for disciplinary and career stage differences. At 55 my hI,norm is relatively high in comparison to my h-index of 69. This is due to the large number of single-authored papers in my h-index. My hIa is also quite high at 2.04. In a study I conducted of some 150 professors at the University of Melbourne, a university that ranks in the top-50 worldwide, there were only a dozen academics with a hI,annual above 1.0. Hence, for most academics the hIa is likely to be *substantially* below 1.0.

At 25 my hA-index shows that I have published 25 papers that have at least 25 citations *per year*. The h-index and the hA-index can easily be "eyeballed" in Publish or Perish by sorting your publications by respectively the number of citations or the number of citations per year and simply "traveling down" the list until the rank in the list matches the number of citations (per year). For the hA-index you can see below how this works.

	Cites	Per year ∨	Rank	Authors	Title	Year
☑ h	1,078	179.67	2	AW Harzing, S Alakangas	Google Scholar, Scopus and the Web of Science: A longitudinal and cross-disc...	2016
☑ h	1,426	95.07	1	AW Harzing	Publish or Perish	2007
☑ h	1,004	77.23	3	NJ Adler, AW Harzing	When knowledge wins: Transcending the sense and nonsense of academic ran...	2009
☑ h	847	60.50	5	AW Harzing, R van der Wal	Google Scholar as a new source for citation analysis?	2008
☑ h	668	55.67	9	AW Harzing, A Pinnington	International Human Resource Management	2010
☑ h	831	51.94	6	AW Harzing	Response styles in cross-national survey research: A 26-country Study	2006
☑ h	518	43.17	15	AW Harzing	The Publish or Perish Book: Your guide to Effective and Responsible Citation A...	2010
☑ h	852	42.60	4	AW Harzing	Acquisitions versus greenfield investments: International strategy and manage...	2002
☑ h	339	42.38	22	H Tenzer, M Pudelko, AW Harzing	The impact of language barriers on trust formation in multinational teams	2014
☑ h	545	41.92	13	N Noorderhaven, AW Harzing	Knowledge-sharing and social interaction within MNEs	2009
☑ h	115	38.33	54	AW Harzing	Two new kids on the block: How do Crossref and Dimensions compare with Go...	2019
☑ h	525	35.00	14	M Pudelko, AW Harzing	Country-of-origin, localization, or dominance effect? An empirical investigatio...	2007
☑ h	204	34.00	35	AW Harzing, M Pudelko, B Sebastian R...	The bridging role of expatriates and inpatriates in knowledge transfer in multin...	2016
☑ h	730	33.18	7	AW Harzing	An empirical analysis and extension of the Bartlett and Ghoshal typology of m...	2000
☑ h	460	32.86	19	AW Harzing, AJ Feely	The language barrier and its implications for HQ-subsidiary relationships	2008
☑ h	678	32.29	8	AW Harzing	Of bears, bumble-bees, and spiders: The role of expatriates in controlling forei...	2001
☑ h	419	32.23	20	AW Harzing, R van der Wal	A Google Scholar h-index for journals: An alternative metric to measure journal...	2009
☑ h	353	32.09	21	AW Harzing, K Köster, U Magner	Babel in business: The language barrier and its solutions in the HQ-subsidiary...	2011
☑ h	160	32.00	46	H Tenzer, S Terjesen, AW Harzing	Language in International Business: A Review and Agenda for Future Research	2017
☑ h	580	30.53	11	AJ Feely, AW Harzing	Language management in multinational companies	2003
☑ h	149	29.80	48	A Martin-Martin, E Orduna-Malea, AW...	Can we use Google Scholar to identify highly-cited documents?	2017
☑ h	253	28.11	29	AW Harzing, M Pudelko	Language competencies, policies and practices in multinational corporations:...	2013
☑ h	506	26.63	16	AW Harzing, A Sorge	The relative impact of country of origin and universal contingencies on interna...	2003
☑ h	607	26.39	10	AW Harzing	Managing the multinationals: An international study of control mechanisms	1999
☑ h	234	26.00	34	AW Harzing	A preliminary test of Google Scholar as a source for citation data: a longitudina...	2013
☑	150	25.00	47	AW Harzing, M Pudelko	Do we need to distance ourselves from the distance concept? Why home and...	2016
☑ h	169	24.14	43	S Reiche, AW Harzing, M Pudelko	Why and how does shared language affect subsidiary knowledge inflows? A so...	2015
☑ h	484	23.05	17	AW Harzing	Who's in charge? An empirical study of executive staffing practices in foreign...	2001

For the next article to enter the hA-index and increase it to 26, it would need to gain 13 citations to make up the necessary 7 (the number of years since publication) times 26 citations. However, at the same time the last article currently captured in the hA-index would need to gather 6 citations to make up 6x26 citations. For the hA to increase to 27, two articles not yet in the hA would need to gain 20 citations (7x27-169) and 83 citations (21x27–484) respectively. Moreover, the four articles that currently have between 25.00 and 26.63 citations per year would need to increase their citations.

This shows how difficult it is for an individual's hA index to increase beyond a certain level. Because of its recency, there hasn't been much research into the hA to date. However, in the University of Melbourne sample I mentioned earlier, there are only six academics with a hA above 20, with half of the sample having a hA of 10 or lower. Remember, this is a group of professors at one of the world's top universities. So don't be disappointed if your hA is quite low.

Given the "strictness" of the hA, we have also implemented a more flexible annual citation metric in Publish or Perish, the ACC. This simply lists the number of papers that have at least 1, 2, 5, 10, or 20 citations per year. This allows academics to pick a metric that puts their record in the best possible light.

In sum

This chapter provided a crash course about data sources and metrics for citation analysis, discussing the Web of Science, Scopus, Google Scholar, and newer data sources, as well as both traditional research metrics (publications, citations, and journal impact factor) and newer research metrics (h-index and alternatives and g-index). It closed by showing how the free Publish or Perish software provides gives you access to all these data sources and metrics.

By providing a choice of data sources and metrics I presented you with a menu of choices allowing you make the best possible case for impact. In Chapter 3 we will look at making your case for impact in a bit more detail, discussing six different strategies.

Chapter 3: How to make your case for citation impact

Many academics use the Publish or Perish software (see Chapter 2) to make a case for tenure, promotion, or prepare for other types of research evaluation. In this chapter, I will provide some pointers on how to report your case for citation impact more effectively. Note that my suggestions refer to citation impact only. They do not relate to the *content* of your research, nor to teaching or service/external engagement activities. For tips on those refer to one of my other books: *Writing effective promotion applications*.

First, please understand that it is *your* job to convince and educate your tenure or promotion panel of the impact of your research. Many senior academics, having grown up in an age in which citations were relatively unimportant, have a limited knowledge of their own or other academics' citation records. Moreover, many academics have the tendency to subconsciously overestimate what their own records were when they went up for tenure or promotion. Hence, they are implicitly using an inappropriate reference group.

If you have an excellent record, you might think it is unfair to have to do all this work to get tenure or promotion. You may also think senior academics should know better. That might well be true, but remember they are only human and are very busy. Moreover, many processes in academia (e.g., any further promotions, job applications, funding applications, research awards, and fellowship applications) depend on you making a case for the impact of your research. Hence it is not a bad idea to get some skills in "selling" your record!

In this chapter, I discuss five strategies. Just pick and mix the ones that suit your record best: pick your metrics wisely, create your own reference group, compare your papers to the journal average, present comprehensive citation counts for edited volumes, and find the pearls in your record. Finally, I also provide some advice on what to do if you have very few citations overall.

1. Pick your metrics wisely

Publish or Perish provides you with a very wide range of metrics. If your university prescribes the metrics you should use, you have little choice. However, in many cases there is more flexibility. So, what metrics do you pick? The screenshot below shows a summary of my own citation record in August 2022. Both my h-index and g-index are relatively high in comparison to other academics in my field, so it is quite easy for me to make my case.

Citation metrics	?		
Publication years:	1995-2022	h-index:	69
Citation years: 27 (1995-2022)		g-index:	154
Papers:	178	hI,norm:	55
Citations:	23957	hI,annual:	2.04
Cites/year:	887.30	hA-index:	25
Cites/paper:	134.59	Papers with ACC ≥ 1,2,5,10,20:	
Authors/paper:	2.02	125,109,80,60,30	

However, if I had a free choice and was applying for a professorial position, I would probably point out that my individual h-index (hI,norm) is relatively high in comparison to my regular h-index. I would also point out my relatively high hI,annual and hA-index, as well as my high ACCs (annualised citation counts). This would allow me to make the case that:

- **My most-cited work is single-authored**. This makes it easy to substantiate that I made a significant intellectual contribution. It also shows that my citation record is not inflated by citations from (famous) co-authors and their networks.

- **I have made a sustained contribution over the years**, reflected in my high hI,annual, i.e. on average I have published more than two single-authored equivalent impactful articles every year in the last 27 years. Most academics will see their hI,annual decline gradually after a mid-career highpoint. It becomes harder to increase your h-index once it is at a fairly high level and without a further increase in the h-index, the hI,annual will decline with each passing year.

- **I have published a significant number of sustainably impactful publications**, reflected by my high hA-index, i.e., I have 25 articles with at least 25 citations per year. This is confirmed by my high ACCs. I have 60 articles with 10 or more citations *per year* and 30 articles with 20 or more citations per year.

Advice for early to mid-career academics

Whether it is beneficial for you to use the individual h-index rather than the regular h-index and g-index depends on your number of highly cited single-authored articles. Note that Publish or Perish will provide you with three implementations of the individual h-index: hI,norm, hI-index, and hm-index; the latter two are only visible when you export the metrics. So, feel free to pick the one that shows of your case to its best advantage!

The hI,annual can be particularly useful if you are an early or mid-career academic as this metric is often relatively high at this career stage. Using the hIa allows you to compare yourself against more senior academics on an equal footing. Of course, you need to inspire confidence that you will be able to sustain this level of performance. It is not easy to keep publishing new impactful articles every year!

2. Create your own reference group

You can make your case for citation impact by comparing your citation record to a *relevant* group of peers. Many evaluators have very little idea of what typical norm scores for the various metrics are. So, unless you make an *explicit* comparison, they will – consciously or subconsciously - use their own reference group. This might not work to your advantage.

There are vast disciplinary differences in typical citations levels. This is especially true when using the Web of Science as a data source (see Chapter 2). Therefore, if your university has tenure or promotion committees that include academics in related, or even unrelated, disciplines, it is even more important to position your case for tenure or promotion within an appropriate reference group. Below I first show how citations can vary dramatically even within sub-disciplines, and then explain how to pick your reference group.

Differences in citation levels within sub-disciplines

The area of Human Resource Management, as a sub-discipline of Management, includes scholars working on industrial relations and labour unions, as well as scholars working on more psychologically oriented topics such as motivation or job attitudes, which is generally classified as organisational behaviour. The latter academics might be able to publish in one of the top mainstream Psychology journals such as *Psychological Bulletin*. The former academics would probably aim for the top US journal in their field: *Industrial Relations*. The journal impact factor of *Psychological Bulletin* is nearly eight times as high as the journal impact factor of *Industrial Relations*.

Moreover, as their research is very contextual, many academics in Industrial Relations will not be able to publish in mainstream US-American Industrial Relations journals. They are likely to publish in lower-impact journals such as *British Journal of Industrial Relations*, *European Journal of Industrial Relations*, or the Australian *Labour History*. Therefore, even within the sub-discipline of HRM, academics in the area of Industrial Relations can be expected to be cited far less frequently than academics in the area of Organisational Behaviour.

The screenshot below shows a Publish or Perish analysis comparing *Psychological Bulletin* with Industrial Relations journals for 2016-2020. It shows how articles in the former can expect much higher citation rates. Even within the set of industrial relations journals there is a clear difference between the well-established British journal, the (much younger) European journal and the very localised Australian journal. Therefore, looking at how your article compares with other articles in the journal is another good strategy (see the next section).

Search terms		Source	Papers	Cites ⌄	Cites/year	h
✓ Psychological Bulletin, ISSN 0033-2909...	G	Google Scholar	206	35,899	5,983.17	109
✓ British Journal of Industrial Relations, IS...	G	Google Scholar	268	4,204	700.67	33
✓ European Journal of Industrial Relations,...	G	Google Scholar	129	2,343	390.50	27
✓ Labour History, ISSN 0023-6942 from 2...	G	Google Scholar	248	53	8.83	3

How to pick your reference group?

It is very important to pick your reference group wisely. It should be narrow enough to reflect any of the differences in citation behaviours across disciplines, sub-disciplines, or even sub-sub-disciplines that we discussed above. However, it should not be so narrow that it leads your committee to discard your selection as either biased or irrelevant. I have found the following two strategies to be particularly effective: a national or international discipline-based strategy and an institution-based strategy.

For the discipline-based strategy, you compare your citation record with a *representative* selection of academics in your field of research at the level you are applying for. Depending on your field, the level you are applying for, and the country you work in, this could be a national or an international group of scholars. To make your case convincing, it is usually best to pick academics at institutions of a similar or higher level of prestige. If you can show that you are performing at the same level as the average of academics in more prestigious institutions who have been in position for a while, you have a very strong case.

The institution-based strategy is a more local strategy. Here you compare your record with academics in your *own* institution at the level you are applying for. If you have access to the length of tenure of your academic colleagues, you might be able to compare your own record with that of both long-established academics and those who were recently promoted to the same level. The former is effective if promotion criteria have not changed over time. The latter might be more effective if they have become more stringent in recent years. More generally, this strategy might be useful if your institution has more stringent norms for promotion than comparable institutions.

I used a combination of both strategies in my promotion application at the University of Melbourne (see table below), comparing my own metrics with recent promotions in the department, professors in the field of International Business in Australia, and more established professors in the department. Note the h-indices and citation levels in this table might appear very low by today's standards. That is because - with publications expanding at 10%/year - average citation levels have increased dramatically in the last 15 years. The general principle of comparison is still valid, however.

Table 1: Bibliometric comparison with other professors, mean and range are given for each indicator.

Group	h-index	1st authored papers in h-index	Single-authored papers in h-index	Number of ISI citing articles (2006 only)	Number of years as professor
2005/2006 promotions	Mean: 6.3 Range: 4-8	Mean: 4.3 Range: 3-5	Mean: 3.0 Range: 2-4	Mean: 15 Range: 3-34	Recently appointed
IB professors at top Oz unis	Mean: 9.0 Range: 4-16	Mean: 3.3 Range: 1-6	Mean: 1.5 Range: 0-3	Mean: 10 Range: 3-21	15 years (4-28 years)
DoMM established professors	Mean: 14.0 Range: 6-22	Mean: 5.0 Range: 0-11	Mean: 2.0 Range: 0-4	Mean: 46 Range: 8-102	14 years (10-19 years)
Anne-Wil Harzing	13	13	10	63	N/A

Please note that you will normally need at least 3-4 academics in your reference group to be able to make a credible comparison. Larger numbers are advisable. I would generally advise against listing the names of individuals as this can easily lead to a hostile response. However, be prepared to substantiate your averages if so requested. You might wish to create folders for your reference groups in the Publish or Perish query centre, so that you can store and update your analyses easily.

3. Compare papers to the journal average

The previous section suggested you pick your own reference group, focusing on academics in your discipline or university. But what better reference group than other articles published at the same time in the same journal? In this section, I will show you how you can make your case for academic research impact by strategically comparing your papers to their journal reference group. To do so simply search for the journal you published in, and set the years to the year of your publication. To make your case you can pursue several avenues.

Most cited paper in the journal that year

The Publish or Perish screenshot below compares my 2001 paper published in *Journal of World Business* with other papers published in the same year. You can see that it is the most highly cited paper in the journal in that particular year and its citations also compared well with the journal average. You could write this up in your case as: *"My 2001 paper in Journal of World Business was the most cited paper out of 25 papers published that year and had nearly four times as many citations as the average paper in the journal that year."*

Most cited single-authored paper

Now of course it won't happen very often that your paper is the most cited article in the journal. So, you can be a bit creative in this as well. The Publish or Perish screenshot below shows my 2000 publication in the *Journal of International Business Studies*.

My paper was not the most cited paper in the journal that year, but it was the 2nd most cited single-authored paper and the 5th most cited paper overall (out of 42), which in a top US journal might be seen as a significant achievement. In my promotion application, I combined this observation with the statement that: *I am one of only two academics affiliated with an Australian university who has ever published a single-authored article in Journal of International Business Studies (JIBS) since it was established 37 years ago.*

If you work outside North America and have published in a North American journal, you could also make an argument that publishing in these journals is more difficult from outside North America. Check whether your paper is the most cited article by a non-North American academic or whether it is the most cited article by an academic from your own country.

Paper in top 5% or top 10% most cited

Of course, it will not happen very often that your paper is one of the most-cited papers in the journal in question. However, even being able to say that it is within the top 5% or top 10% most cited papers that year would make a very significant contribution to your case.

If you are lucky, you might have articles that are amongst the most-cited articles in a particular journal over a longer period. If you could say that your article was among the top 5% or top 10% most cited articles in a particular journal over its entire history of publication that would make a very strong case, especially if the journal was a particularly well-known journal.

	Cites	Per year	Rank	Authors	Title	Year
☑ h	7,047	414.53	1	AY Kolb, DA Kolb	Learning styles and learning spaces: Enhancing experiential learning in higher education	2005
☑ h	5,362	315.41	2	S Ghoshal	Bad management theories are destroying good management practices	2005
☑ h	2,576	128.80	3	J Pfeffer, CT Fong	The end of business schools? Less success than meets the eye	2002
☑ h	1,374	98.14	4	F Luthans, JB Avey, JL Patera	Experimental analysis of a web-based training intervention to develop positive psycho...	2008
☑ h	1,288	71.56	5	B Honig	Entrepreneurship education: Toward a model of contingency-based business planning	2004
☑ h	1,229	76.81	6	D Dunne, R Martin	Design thinking and how it will change management education: An interview and discus...	2006
☑ h	1,217	110.64	7	RJ Ely, H Ibarra, DM Kolb	Taking gender into account: Theory and design for women's leadership development pr...	2011
☑ h	1,111	61.72	8	PC Earley, RS Peterson	The elusive cultural chameleon: Cultural intelligence as a new approach to intercultural...	2004
☑ h	1,023	204.60	10	G Nabi, F Liñán, A Fayolle, N Kru...	The impact of entrepreneurship education in higher education: A systematic review and...	2017
☑	1,004	77.23	9	NJ Adler, AW Harzing	When knowledge wins: Transcending the sense and nonsense of academic rankings	2009
☑ h	919	57.44	11	DL McCabe, KD Butterfield...	Academic dishonesty in graduate business programs: Prevalence, causes, and propose...	2006
☑ h	914	45.70	12	DC Kayes	Experiential learning and its critics: Preserving the role of experience in management le...	2002
☑ h	910	50.56	13	DR DeTienne, GN Chandler	Opportunity identification and its role in the entrepreneurial classroom: A pedagogical a...	2004
☑ h	833	64.08	14	KY Ng, L Van Dyne, S Ang	From experience to experiential learning: Cultural intelligence as a learning capability fo...	2009
☑ h	784	39.20	15	RE Boyatzis, EC Stubbs, SN Tayl...	Learning cognitive and emotional intelligence competencies through graduate manage...	2002
☑ h	782	39.10	16	C Argyris	Double-loop learning, teaching, and research	2002

My 2009 article with Nancy Adler in the *Academy of Management Learning & Education* was in the top 1% of articles (10th out of more than 1,000 papers) published in AMLE since its inception in 2002 with a total of 1,000 (Google Scholar) citations (see above). This would be a strong claim for its impact.

However, it is not such a good idea to use this strategy if your paper was published early in the period you are reporting on. For instance, if you claim that your paper is amongst the 25% most cited articles in a journal between 2000-2022, and your paper was published in 2000/2001, it is likely that your paper was cited less than average for articles published in 2000 and 2001.

Sorting publications by the number of citations per year (the second column) is a good way to avoid this problem as this automatically corrects for the age of the article. If we sort the above screenshot on citations per year, my article with Nancy moves up to #8 and several recent contributions, published between 2015 and 2020, now rank much higher in the list.

Compare a body of work

If you do not have any papers that really stand out, but your papers are generally well cited in comparison to the journals they are published in, you could emphasise this. For instance, you could say something like: *"on average my articles are amongst the top 20%-30% most cited papers when compared to papers published in the same journal in the same year"*.

You will need to be a little careful with this strategy though. Unless you have some papers that have been published in journals that your evaluation committee will recognise as top journals, it will only elicit the comment that you tend to "waste your work" by publishing in low impact journals. So, you may need to combine this strategy with some evidence that the journals you have published in have high standards of peer review.

4. Present comprehensive citation counts for edited volumes

In some disciplines it is common to publish edited volumes. In these cases, the volume's editor might need to invest considerable effort coaching its contributors to submit their chapters in time, and typically also provides significant editorial input. Edited volumes can also make a major contribution to the field as they often provide a collection of the latest research on a particular topic. Unfortunately, edited volumes are often not appreciated as much as monographs or journal articles. Their citation impact might also be modest.

However, one reason for this modest citation count might be that few academics will refer to the edited volume as a whole. Authors more commonly refer to individual chapters *within* an edited volume. Moreover, some edited volumes, such as handbooks or companions go through various editions. Thus, collating the citation counts of the individual chapters and editions will provide a more comprehensive case of the publication's its impact.

Worked example: IHRM textbook

In 1995, I published an edited textbook on the topic of International Human Resource Management, with new editions published in 2004, 2010, 2014, 2019, and 2022. Although it was a textbook, Publish or Perish demonstrates that it generated quite a lot of citations in the academic literature. Many of these citations were to the book as a whole, with a combined number of some 700 citations for the various editions.

However, as the three screenshots below show, there were a further 535 citations to individual chapters in the 1994/1995 edition, 880 to chapters the 2004 edition and 280 to chapters in the 2010/2011 edition. Overall, the book thus had nearly 2,500 citations, a number that would allow me to more easily argue the case that this edited volume has had a very significant impact in the field of International Human Resource Management.

Google Scholar search					Citation metrics	?
Authors:		Years: 1994 - 1995	Search	?	Publication years:	1994-1995
Publication name:	International Human Resource Management	ISSN:	Search Direct		Citation years: 28 (1994-2022)
					Papers:	14
Title words:			Clear All		Citations:	535

Google Scholar search					Citation metrics	?
Authors:		Years: 2004 - 2004	Search	?	Publication years:	2004-2004
Publication name:	International Human Resource Management	ISSN:	Search Direct		Citation years: 18 (2004-2022)
					Papers:	18
Title words:			Clear All		Citations:	880

Google Scholar search					Citation metrics	?
Authors:		Years: 2010 - 2011	Search	?	Publication years:	2010-2011
Publication name:	International Human Resource Management	ISSN:	Search Direct		Citation years: 12 (2010-2022)
					Papers:	13
Title words:			Clear All		Citations:	280

Interestingly, Google Scholar didn't show any significant citations to the 2014, 2019, and 2022 editions. This might have been caused by a Google Scholar flaw that attributes book citations to the wrong version. In this example, this is immaterial as our aim was to provide a comprehensive count for various editions combined.

5. Find the pearls in your record

The most important realisation in presenting your case for tenure, promotion, or grant applications is that every case is different. We all have "pearls" in our research portfolio. You just need to find and polish them, so they shine brightly. Of course, sometimes you are prescribed to list a number of metrics, maybe total citation counts, or h-index, or your number of publications. However, even in that case you can always add additional information.

Different profiles, different stories

Over a decade ago, I had a colleague at the University of Melbourne – Maria Kraimer – whose total Google Scholar citation level was very similar to mine. Even now our total citations are less than 6% apart and as she started publishing 2 years later, our citations/per year counts are virtually identical. However, I would suggest two very different ways of presenting our records to our best advantage.

Ground-breaking contributions

As Maria, I would indicate that I had no less than five articles that have gathered 100 or more citations per year. I would also point out that four of my articles have gathered more than 2,000 citations and six more than 1,000 (see screenshot below), indicating they are truly ground-breaking. I would also mention that I had made these ground-breaking contributions very early in my career; Maria's seven most highly cited articles were all published shortly after her PhD completion.

	Cites	Per year	Rank	Authors	Title	Year
☑ h	3,484	165.90	1	SE Seibert, ML Kraimer, RC Liden	A social capital theory of career success	2001
☑ h	2,671	127.19	2	RT Sparrowe, RC Liden, SJ Way...	Social networks and the performance of individuals and groups	2001
☑ h	2,333	101.43	3	SE Seibert, JM Crant, ML Kraimer	Proactive personality and career success.	1999
☑ h	2,099	99.95	4	SE Seibert, ML Kraimer, JM Crant	What do proactive people do? A longitudinal model linking proactive personality and car...	2001
☑ h	1,262	60.10	5	SE Seibert, ML Kraimer	The five-factor model of personality and career success	2001
☑ h	1,010	48.10	6	ML Kraimer, SJ Wayne, RAA Ja...	Sources of support and expatriate performance: The mediating role of expatriate adjust...	2001
☑ h	796	34.61	7	SJ Wayne, RC Liden, ML Kraime...	The role of human capital, motivation and supervisor sponsorship in predicting career s...	1999
☑ h	743	41.28	8	B Erdogan, ML Kraimer, RC Liden	Work value congruence and intrinsic career success: The compensatory roles of leader...	2004
☑ h	659	41.19	9	B Erdogan, RC Liden, ML Kraimer	Justice and leader-member exchange: The moderating role of organizational culture	2006
☑ h	652	36.22	10	ML Kraimer, SJ Wayne	An examination of perceived organizational support as a multidimensional construct in t...	2004
☑ h	620	56.36	11	ML Kraimer, SE Seibert, SJ Way...	Antecedents and outcomes of organizational support for development: The critical role...	2011
☑ h	604	60.40	12	MA Shaffer, ML Kraimer, YP Che...	Choices, challenges, and career consequences of global work experiences: A review an...	2012
☑ h	528	22.96	13	ML Kraimer, SE Seibert, RC Liden	Psychological empowerment as a multidimensional construct: A test of construct validity	1999
☑ h	434	22.84	14	RC Liden, SJ Wayne, ML Kraime...	The dual commitments of contingent workers: An examination of contingents' commitm...	2003
☑ h	359	179.50	15	J Akkermans, J Richardson, ML...	The Covid-19 crisis as a career shock: Implications for careers and vocational behavior	2020

I would probably not discuss co-authorship patterns in any detail as this is not a particular strength of Maria's record. Many of her highly cited publications were lead-authored by someone else. One could of course consider pointing to well-known co-authors, but this is a bit of a double-edged sword. To some readers this is a very positive sign, others might wonder about the academic's own contribution.

Sustained and single-authored contributions

As Anne-Wil, I would make a very different case, given that I do not have any articles with extremely high citation levels (i.e., above 2,000). Although I do have three publications that have more than 1,000 citations, none of these are in my main research area (International Business). I would, however, indicate that I have no less than 25 articles that have each gathered more than 25 or more citations per year (see screenshot below).

		Cites	Per year ∨	Rank	Authors	Title	Year
☑	h	1,073	178.83	2	AW Harzing, S Alakan...	Google Scholar, Scopus and the Web of Science: A longitudinal and...	2016
☑	h	1,420	94.67	1	AW Harzing	Publish or Perish	2007
☑	h	1,002	77.08	3	NJ Adler, AW Harzing	When knowledge wins: Transcending the sense and nonsense of a...	2009
☑	h	845	60.36	5	AW Harzing, R van der...	Google Scholar as a new source for citation analysis?	2008
☑	h	668	55.67	9	AW Harzing, A Pinning...	International Human Resource Management	2010
☑	h	832	52.00	6	AW Harzing	Response styles in cross-national survey research: A 26-country St...	2006
☑	h	515	42.92	15	AW Harzing	The Publish or Perish Book: Your guide to Effective and Responsibl...	2010
☑	h	851	42.55	4	AW Harzing	Acquisitions versus greenfield investments: International strategy a...	2002
☑	h	337	42.13	22	H Tenzer, M Pudelko,...	The impact of language barriers on trust formation in multinational...	2014
☑	h	545	41.92	13	N Noorderhaven, AW...	Knowledge-sharing and social interaction within MNEs	2009
☑	h	114	38.00	55	AW Harzing	Two new kids on the block: How do Crossref and Dimensions comp...	2019
☑	h	525	35.00	14	M Pudelko, AW Harzing	Country-of-origin, localization, or dominance effect? An empirical i...	2007
☑	h	204	34.00	35	AW Harzing, M Pudelk...	The bridging role of expatriates and inpatriates in knowledge transf...	2016
☑	h	730	33.18	7	AW Harzing	An empirical analysis and extension of the Bartlett and Ghoshal typ...	2000
☑	h	459	32.79	19	AW Harzing, AJ Feely	The language barrier and its implications for HQ-subsidiary relation...	2008
☑	h	678	32.29	8	AW Harzing	Of bears, bumble-bees, and spiders: The role of expatriates in cont...	2001
☑	h	419	32.23	20	AW Harzing, R van der...	A Google Scholar h-index for journals: An alternative metric to mea...	2009
☑	h	353	32.09	21	AW Harzing, K Köster,...	Babel in business: The language barrier and its solutions in the HQ-...	2011
☑	h	159	31.80	46	H Tenzer, S Terjesen,...	Language in International Business: A Review and Agenda for Futur...	2017
☑	h	578	30.42	11	AJ Feely, AW Harzing	Language management in multinational companies	2003
☑	h	149	29.80	48	A Martin-Martin, E Or...	Can we use Google Scholar to identify highly-cited documents?	2017
☑	h	253	28.11	29	AW Harzing, M Pudelko	Language competencies, policies and practices in multinational cor...	2013
☑	h	503	26.47	16	AW Harzing, A Sorge	The relative impact of country of origin and universal contingencies...	2003
☑	h	606	26.35	10	AW Harzing	Managing the multinationals: An international study of control mec...	1999
☑	h	234	26.00	34	AW Harzing	A preliminary test of Google Scholar as a source for citation data: a...	2013
☑	h	150	25.00	47	AW Harzing, M Pudelko	Do we need to distance ourselves from the distance concept? Why...	2016

I would also point out that my most highly cited work is largely first or single-authored and that much of it was published in the second half of my career, thus indicating that my impact has not slowed down after being promoted to Full Professor in 2006. That said, I would probably also emphasise that my PhD thesis (Managing the Multinationals, 3rd from below) has turned out to be quite influential.

Creating effective stories

So, my story and that of Maria would be very different, despite our similar citation levels. As I indicated in the introduction of my 2010 Publish or Perish book.

> *Citations are not only a reflection of the impact that a particular piece of academic work has generated. Citations can also be used to tell stories about academics, journals, and fields of research. This book is meant to help you create effective stories.*

So go ahead: find the pearls in your record, polish them and string them into a beautifully arranged necklace that presents your citation story effectively.

6. What if you have very few citations?

Of course, it is rather difficult to make your case for citation impact if you have very few citations overall. This will often be the case if you are a junior researcher who has started publishing quite recently. In this instance, there are three things you can do beyond making the general argument that citation scores in your discipline are low as we discussed in Section 2 (only if that's the case of course).

Argue for the use of Google Scholar

First, if your University prefers the Web of Science as a data source and you have very few citations in the Web of Science, but quite a respectable number of citations in Google Scholar, you can argue that Google Scholar citations are a more accurate measurement of citation impact for junior scholars.

This is true because Google Scholar includes citations in Masters and Doctoral theses, conference proceedings and working papers that, in most cases, will ultimately be reflected in Web of Science citations. As we discussed in Chapter 2, Google Scholar also includes books, book chapters, and a wider range of journals than Web of Science, especially in the Social Sciences and Humanities.

Argue citations are slow to pick up

Second, explain that citations can take a long time to pick up. This is particularly true for the Social Sciences and Humanities, where the publication process is generally more drawn-out with many rounds of revisions. Even accepted publications can take a very long time to finally appear in print. In contrast, in disciplines such as Molecular Biology & Genetics or Astrophysics the time lapse between research and publication and publication and citation is generally much shorter. Hence, whereas one can expect a PhD student or postdoc in these fields to have citations, this is rarely ever the case in the Social Sciences and Humanities.

My current Web of Science citation record puts me in the top 1% most cited academics in my field and I receive around 1,400 new Web of Science citations a year. However, my citations took rather a long time to take off. My first publication appeared in 1995 and by 2000 I had about a dozen publications printed or in press/accepted. However, at the start of 2000 I only had nine Web of Science citations (with 20 new citations in 2000 and 27 new citations in 2001). If I had had to make my tenure case after just 5 years, I wouldn't have had much to show for in terms of research impact!

You might be able to apply this strategy by doing some analyses for top people in your field and look at their first five years after they published their first article. This strategy is probably most effective when combined with the next strategy.

Argue for quality "by association"

Third, if you have only a few citations, it might be worth tracking each of them down to find out who is citing your work. It is more impressive if some famous academics in your field have cited work, or if many of your citations occur in the top journals in your field. Some of the fame and quality image of the academics and journals citing your work might rub off on you in the eyes of your evaluation committee.

	Cites ⌄	Per year	Rank	Authors	Title		Year
✓	1,420	94.67	1	AW Harzing	Publish or Perish	Open Article in Browser	07
✓ h	1,073	178.83	2	AW Harzing, S Alakan...	Google Scholar, Scoƿ		16
✓ h	1,002	77.08	3	NJ Adler, AW Harzing	When knowledge wir	Open Full Text in Browser	09
✓ h	851	42.55	4	AW Harzing	Acquisitions versus ǥ	Open Citing Works in Browser	02
✓ h	845	60.36	5	AW Harzing, R van der...	Google Scholar as a	Open Related Works in Browser	08
✓ h	832	52.00	6	AW Harzing	Response styles in cɪ	Retrieve Citing Works in Publish or Perish	06
✓ h	730	33.18	7	AW Harzing	An empirical analysis	Find Article with Unpaywall	00
✓ h	678	32.29	8	AW Harzing	Of bears, bumble-be		01
✓ h	668	55.67	9	AW Harzing, A Pinning...	International Human	Split Citations	10
✓ h	606	26.35	10	AW Harzing	Managing the multin;		99
✓ h	578	30.42	11	AJ Feely, AW Harzing	Language managemє	Copy Results >	03
✓ h	559	20.70	12	AW Harzing	The persistent myth	Save Results >	95
✓ h	545	41.92	13	N Noorderhaven, AW...	Knowledge-sharing ɛ		09
✓ h	525	35.00	14	M Pudelko, AW Harzing	Country-of-origin, lo	Select All ⌘ A	07
✓ h	515	42.92	15	AW Harzing	The Publish or Perisɦ	Check All	10
✓ h	503	26.47	16	AW Harzing, A Sorge	The relative impact c	Check Selection	03
✓ h	484	23.05	17	AW Harzing	Who's in charge? An		01
✓ h	481	19.24	18	AW Harzing	Response rates in int	Uncheck All	97
✓ h	459	32.79	19	AW Harzing, AJ Feely	The language barrier	Uncheck Selection	08
✓ h	419	32.23	20	AW Harzing, R van der...	A Google Scholar h-i	Uncheck 0 Cites	09
✓ h	353	32.09	21	AW Harzing, K Köster,...	Babel in business: Tɦ	Uncheck CITATION Results	11
✓ h	337	42.13	22	H Tenzer, M Pudelko,...	The impact of language barriers on trust formation in multinational...	2014
✓ h	309	16.26	23	AW Harzing	The role of culture in entry-mode studies: from neglect to myopia?	2003

Quality of citing works

To find out who is citing your work and where, right-click on the publication in question and click "**Retrieve Citing Works in Publish or Perish**" (see screenshot above). Publish or Perish will now retrieve all citing works. Currently, this option is only available for Google Scholar, Google Scholar Profiles and Open Alex.

You can also do this for a set of articles. The screenshot below shows the results of a citing works search for the seven articles I published in the *Journal of International Business Studies*. As you can see in the screenshot below – which shows the first 10 citing works – I limited the search to citations from 2016 onwards to retrieve only recent citations. To find out the journals in which your work is cited simply sort the results by journal. Note that to change the Display title and the years you are searching for, you will need to stop the search. You can then edit these fields and resume the search.

Google Scholar citing references

Display title:	Citations for seven articles in JIBS			Years: 2016 - 0	Retrieve	?
Cited works:	An empirical analysis and extension of the Bartlett and Ghoshal typology of multinational companies				Retrieve Direct	
	Knowledge-sharing and social interaction within MNEs				Apply	
	The impact of language barriers on trust formation in multinational teams					
	The role of international assignees' social capital in creating inter-unit intellectual capital: A cross-level model				Revert	
	Why do international assignees stay? An organizational embeddedness perspective				New	

Cites ˅		Per year	Rank	Authors	Title	Year
☑ h	250	83.33	3	DG Collings, K Mellahi, WF Ca...	Global talent management and performance in multinational enterprises: A mul...	2019
☑ h	162	32.40	4	M Andresen, F Bergdolt	A systematic literature review on the definitions of global mindset and cultural...	2017
☑ h	145	36.25	5	T Kostova, PC Nell, AK Hoenen	Understanding agency problems in headquarters-subsidiary relationships in m...	2018
☑ h	142	28.40	6	PM Wright, MD Ulrich	A road well traveled: The past, present, and future journey of strategic human...	2017
☑ h	140	70.00	7	KE Meyer, C Li, APJ Schotter	Managing the MNE subsidiary: Advancing a multi-level and dynamic research...	2020
☑ h	131	21.83	8	S Morris, S Snell, I Björkman	An architectural framework for global talent management	2016
☑ h	107	21.40	9	JE Tulung	Resource availability and firm's international strategy as key determinants of e...	2017
☑ h	96	16.00	10	D Cerrato, L Crosato, D Depp...	Archetypes of SME internationalization: A configurational approach	2016
☑ h	79	15.80	11	R Grünig, D Morschett	Developing international strategies	2017
☑ h	75	12.50	12	H Mun, HC Moon	The strategy for Korea's economic success	2016

Quality of journal outlets

If you cannot find any famous scholars citing your work, you could instead focus on the quality of the journals that your work appeared in. In general, this is not appropriate, as some papers in top journals never get cited. However, *on average* papers in top journals do get cited more than papers in lower-ranked journals. That's why these journals have higher Journal Impact Factors. Therefore, if your work has been published in high-impact journals, you could make the case that it is *more likely* that your work will be highly cited in the future.

In addition, you could make the argument that these journals have generally higher quality standards for the work they publish and a more rigorous review process. However, that's a quality argument, not a citation impact argument, and although the two are related, as we have seen in Chapter 1, they are not necessarily identical.

Highly influential citations

Finally, you could use Semantic Scholar to track down all citations to your work that are "highly influential" (see also Chapter 2). This may allow you to spot high profile academics or important articles that have built significantly on your work. Obviously, this would be a very time-consuming exercise for senior scholars with many citations, and thus a substantial number of "highly influential" citations. However, for a junior academic with only a dozen highly influential citation, it could be very useful to find out which articles were highly influenced by your own work.

In sum

In this chapter I showed you how you can make your case for citation impact, discussing five specific strategies: picking your metrics wisely, creating your own reference group, comparing your papers to the journal average, presenting comprehensive citation counts for edited volumes, and finding the pearls in your record. Finally, I also provided some advice on what to do if you have very few citations overall.

In the next chapter we'll look at the other side of the coin: evaluating research impact. We will discuss the two key alternatives to evaluate research impact: peer review and metrics.

Chapter 4: Evaluating impact: peer review vs metrics

After discussing how to *measure* (Chapter 2) and *evidence* (Chapter 3) research impact, this chapter discusses the two main approaches of *evaluating* impact: peer review and metrics. Both alternatives have their own strengths and weaknesses, which is why I would recommend using a combination to evaluate research impact.

In principle, this should not be a problem. As academics we are used to evaluating a problem from different, and even opposing, perspectives. Academic research – especially research in the Social Sciences – is never about black and white, it is about the various shades of grey. Ask an academic a question – any question – and their most likely answer will be: "it depends". We take great care to avoid black-and-white views and straw man arguments, i.e., the distortion of an opposing stance to make it easier to attack.

And yet... in research evaluation the proponents of peer review and metrics do seems to withdraw in opposing camps, unwilling to listen to each other. Those in the "peer review camp" discard metrics out of hand. Those in the "metrics camp" seem to have a blind faith in the accuracy of metrics. Moreover, straw man arguments are commonplace, especially in the peer review camp. So, this chapter will look at the two alternatives in a bit more detail.

Peer review: ideal and reality

Webster dictionary defines peer review as "*a process by which something proposed (as for research or publications) is evaluated by a group of experts in the appropriate field*". Many academics see peer review as the "Gold Standard" of research evaluation and oppose strongly to the use of metrics. However, in doing so they often seem to contrast an idealistic view of peer review with an overly reductionist – strawman – view of metrics, making it easy to reject metrics out of hand.

In an *ideal* world, peer review consists of evaluation by informed, dedicated, and unbiased experts, who have unlimited time at their hands. It is doubtful this ideal world ever existed; it certainly doesn't in today's pressured academic world. Peer review is far from perfect. Many studies have found correlations between peer reviewers' assessment of the same manuscript to be low (see for instance Starbuck (2005): *How Much Better Are the Most-Prestigious Journals?*). Several experimental studies found already published papers to be rejected when resubmitted (see for instance Peters and Ceci's (1982): *The fate of published articles, submitted again.*)

I would argue that the likely *reality* of peer review is an evaluation carried out by hurried semi-experts whose assessment of research quality is – either consciously or subconsciously – influenced by the country in which the research was conducted, the author's university affiliation, as well as demographic characteristics such as gender and race. Where peer review concerns published worked – as in national research evaluations such as the UK's Research Excellence Framework – these biases are compounded by the halo effect of the journal in which the article was published.

At the same time, the alternative – evaluation by metrics – is often discarded using strawman arguments that typically rely on what are called anecdata: anecdotal evidence based on personal observations or opinions, or random investigations, but presented as facts. As academics we are quick to condemn the (wo)man in the street for using anecdata when talking about topics such as migration, vaccination, and climate change.

Many academics seem quite happy, however, to use anecdata in support of their argumentation that metrics should be condemned to the scrapheap. Their arguments usually run along these lines: *"My best article isn't highly cited. So, all metrics are flawed"* or *"So-and-so published a really poor study, but it is on a sexy topic, so it is highly cited. This proves that citations can never be trusted"*. To me this is the equivalent of *"My grandma was smoking a packet of cigarettes a day and lived to be 90"*. Yes, the anecdote might well be true, but that doesn't mean that it can be generalised to *every* individual paper or *every* individual academic.

As academics we know this, don't we? So, can we please do what we do best? Read or conduct some actual research before we proclaim to know what we are talking about. Empirical studies (see e.g., Traag and Waltman (2019): *Systematic analysis of agreement between metrics and peer review in the UK REF*) do point to metrics being highly correlated with peer review, especially at higher levels of analysis such as institutions. They also correlate significantly with promotions and external measures of esteem such as prestigious awards. Yes, there are always exceptions, but we would not question one of our core theories based on one outlier, would we? Ever heard of the saying: The exception proves the rule?

Metrics: reductionistic or inclusive

Research evaluation by metrics nearly always relies on citation-based metrics. As we have discussed in the previous chapter, this could be raw citation counts, but also composite metrics such as the h-index, or field corrected metrics such as the hIa.

When comparing metrics with peer review, metrics are often defined in reductionist terms, focusing only on the Web of Science as a data source and the journal impact factor or the h-index as metrics. Using these definitions, metrics are easily discarded for "ideal world" peer review. However, a more inclusive data source and metrics might compare far better to the likely *reality* of peer review.

Data sources

It is true that the Web of Science doesn't cover many publication outlets that are important in the Social Sciences and Humanities. But that simply means we need to use another data source that does, such as Google Scholar. In my own research – based on a comparison of some 150 carefully matched academics in five distinct disciplines – I have shown that if you do, citations levels for academics in the Social Sciences, Humanities and Engineering are much closer to those of academics in the Natural and Life Sciences (see below).

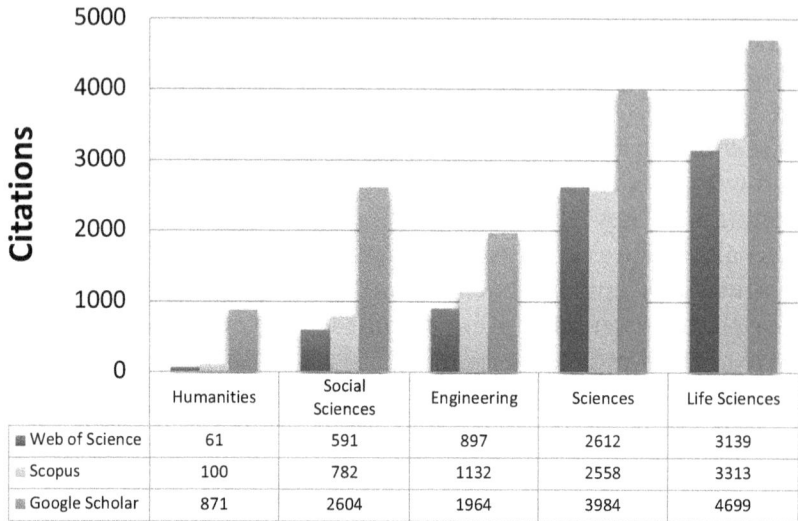

	Humanities	Social Sciences	Engineering	Sciences	Life Sciences
Web of Science	61	591	897	2612	3139
Scopus	100	782	1132	2558	3313
Google Scholar	871	2604	1964	3984	4699

The Web of Science provides the lowest number of citations in each discipline, with Scopus providing a slightly higher count for most disciplines. Google Scholar, as the most comprehensive data source provides the highest number of citations for each of the disciplines. However, what is crucial is that the difference *between* the disciplines is much lower for Google Scholar than for the two other data sources, with the Humanities and Social Sciences in particular benefitting from Google Scholar's much broader coverage. This includes a larger number of journals in these fields, but also books, book chapters and other types of publications.

Whereas for the Web of Science citations in the Life Sciences are more than 50 times as high as for the Humanities and 5 times as high for the Social Sciences, this difference is reduced to 5 times (instead of 50 times) as much for the Humanities and less than twice as much for the Social Sciences (instead of 5 times as much).

Another way of looking at this is comparing the difference between Web of Science and Google Scholar citations between disciplines. For the Life Sciences and Sciences, Google Scholar provides 1.5 times as many citations as the Web of Science, for Engineering this is more than twice as much. For the Social Sciences this is 4.5 times as much and for the Humanities a staggering 14 times as much.

Metrics

When referring to the use of metrics in research evaluation, most of the criticism is targeted at the Web of Science Journal Impact Factor. Indeed, the Journal Impact Factor has many flaws (see also Chapter 2) and should never be used as a measure of the worth of individual publications or academics. In addition, metrics such as the h-index and citations cannot be compared across disciplines or career stages. There is a whole cottage industry of publications – both journal articles and books – pointing this out again and again.

But why throw the baby out with the bathwater? Why not simply use metrics that correct for these differences in field and career stage. The individual annualised h-index which I created, and which can easily be calculated with the free Publish or Perish software (see Chapter 2) corrects for both disciplinary and career stage differences.

The graph below – based on a comparison of some 150 carefully matched academics in five distinct disciplines – shows that the average h-index for a professor in the Life Sciences (33.4) is very similar to that in the Sciences (30.1). However, even though we are using an inclusive data source – Google Scholar – it is nearly three times as high as for a Professor in the Humanities (12.3) and more than 1.5 times as high as in the Social Sciences (21.5) and Engineering (20.8).

Different metrics across disciplines

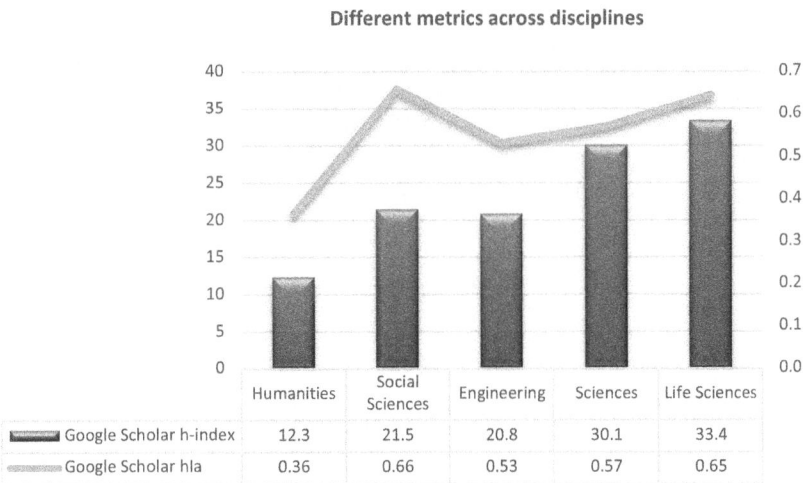

	Humanities	Social Sciences	Engineering	Sciences	Life Sciences
Google Scholar h-index	12.3	21.5	20.8	30.1	33.4
Google Scholar hla	0.36	0.66	0.53	0.57	0.65

If we use an individualised and annualised h-index instead – one that corrects for differences in the number of co-authors and different career lengths – these differences are much smaller. In fact, four of the five disciplines now show very similar indices, with the Social Sciences equalling the Life Sciences. Only the Humanities still shows lower metrics. However, rather than the Humanities score being a third of the Life Sciences as for the h-index, it is now more than half of the Life Sciences.

So going from a comparison of citations in the Web of Science where the Life Sciences outperformed the Humanities with a factor of 50, i.e., 50 times as many citations, this has now been reduced to less than 2, i.e., an individualised annualised h-index in Google Scholar that is nearly twice as high in the Life Sciences when compared to the Humanities. For the Social Sciences the change in relative metrics was very significant too, going from a factor of 5, i.e., citations in the Life Sciences being 5 times as high as in the Social Sciences, to having an annualised individual h-index equal to the Life Sciences.

We should remain careful in comparing metrics across disciplines. However, if we *do* need to compare them, using comprehensive data sources and metrics that correct for different publications and citation practices are essential.

Finally, despite my plea to consider metrics in addition to peer review, I would always recommend a "common sense check". Google Scholar Profiles can be polluted and author disambiguation in the Web of Science isn't flawless either (see also my blogpost: "*Health Warning: Might Contain Multiple Personalities*"). In addition, there are several key aspects of an academic publication and citation record – such as the extent of lead authorship or the number of recent publications - that are not reflected in these high-level metrics.

So... peer review or metrics? Use both!

Unlike some academics appear to believe, metrics are not inherently evil. Academics that are fundamentally opposed to the use of metrics often compare an idealist version of peer review (i.e., conducted by informed, dedicated, unbiased experts) with a reductionist version of metrics (i.e., Web of Science h-index or citations).

In reality, peer review suffers from significant problems, including a lack of agreement between reviewers and biased evaluation. Therefore, a metrics-informed peer-review process could counteract the gender/ethnic/language/disciplinary biases in peer review. So, combining peer review and metrics would always be my preference.

However, if I *had* to choose between inclusive metrics and real-world peer review, my bet would be on metrics. Judging from the many user surveys I get for Publish or Perish (see Chapter 2) I am not the only one! Many academics use it to counter what one of them called "academic buffoons". These are academics whose position is based mainly on connections, favourable demographics, and strong narrative and impression management skills, rather than strong research performance.

I am not saying that citations metrics are immune to bias, metrics are subject to many of the same biases that are present in peer review. But at least metrics are based on the "crowd-sourced opinion" of a large *cross-section* of academics, rather than the view of a smallish group of academics who – in many cases – belong to the privileged majority. In fact, one could argue that metrics are in fact a form of peer review. Although the reasons for citing a paper are varied, at least one of them is that the citing author considers the paper to be of a sufficient quality to use in justifying a particular argument.

So, rather than resorting to the black and white, can we go back to what academics do best: explore the greys and consider carefully when metrics might be helpful, whether in combination with peer review or on their own? We really need to go back to our academic roots: "it depends" should be our standard answer to the question "peer review or metrics?" too.

In sum

In this chapter, we reviewed the two key alternatives for evaluating research impact: peer review and metrics. We argued that academics discarding metrics out of hand are often comparing an ideal world version of peer review with a reductionist version of metrics, such as the WoS Journal Impact Factor. A more inclusive version of metrics, such as the Google Scholar individual annualised h-index can play a useful role in research evaluation.

In the next two chapters, we will switch our focus from *measuring*, *evidencing*, and *evaluating* research impact to *improving* our research impact. First, we'll discuss the four Cs of getting cited in Chapter 5. Then in Chapter 6, I will outline seven steps you can undertake to ensure your paper gets the impact it deserves.

Chapter 5: The four Cs of getting cited

In previous chapters, we have defined the concept of research impact and delineated it from related concepts (Chapter 1), provided an overview of key data sources and metrics and explained how to access them in the Publish or Perish software (Chapter 2). We outlined six strategies to make your case for citation impact in contexts such as promotion and tenure applications (Chapter 3) and looked at the role of peer review vs metrics in research evaluation more generally (Chapter 4). In this chapter we change our focus from *measuring, evidencing,* and *evaluating* citation impact to *improving* citation impact.

I will discuss the four Cs of getting cited: competence, collaboration, care, and communication. This doesn't mean I advocate an instrumental approach to getting cited. What I *am* advocating is ensuring that your publications – which have taken you a lot of "blood, sweat and tears" to complete – do get the impact they deserve. As we have seen in Chapter 1, the term impact can represent a wide range of meanings. This chapter deals with *academic* impact as measured by citations, although many of the recommendations below might also assist in achieving greater *societal* impact.

Why is citation impact important?

Why would you even care about citations? Well, why on earth would you publish if nobody cites your work? Not publishing is a bit like being mute, but not being cited is like talking without anyone talking back. It is very much a one-way conversation. I know I have sometimes compared academics to artists; both are driven by a passion to independently realise our own visions. Hence, there are some artists and academics who mainly care about expressing themselves, not about how others see their work. However, I suspect that even these artists and academics would prefer it if at least some people engaged with their work.

Academic research should contribute to academic *discourse* and citations are part of that discourse. They are a signal other academics are "talking back" to you. Now, you might well say: I know my work is reaching students, managers, or policy makers. That means you are having an impact in your teaching and external engagement role (see Chapter 1). Both roles are important in academia. However, these audiences are not normally our *primary* audience if we are publishing in academic journals. If they were, we would be publishing in very different outlets; outlets that they would read. So, I think you should care about citations because they are a clear signal that your research is contributing to the academic discourse.

But there are three other reasons too. As we discussed in Chapter 3, knowing that your work is cited also helps you to prepare for your confirmation or tenure application, for your promotion application, for your yearly performance appraisal, and more generally your case for academic impact. Being at least somewhat familiar with citation analysis also makes it easier to "educate" your Dean – or other senior academics who might influence your future – on this topic.

Most importantly, citations tell you who is *building* on the work you have done. It is exciting to see how others are using your research. When you start out in academia you are excited simply to publish and see your name in print. However, that excitement fades after a while. Personally, I was far more excited about my first citations as they told me that other academics were reading my work and found it useful. Through understanding how other people use your work, you might also get new ideas for research yourself. Finally, some of the academics citing your work might well be future collaborators. They are clearly interested in your work. Hence, they might want to collaborate with you to take the research agenda forward.

Finally, citations – which occur far more frequently than publications – are a nice ego boost. It is nice to know someone has (presumably) read your work and found it important enough to reference it. They are a regular reminder that the work we are doing has an impact and who doesn't like being reminded of that?

How to improve the chance of getting cited?

Now you know why citation impact is important, what can you do to improve the chances your work is cited. This where the four Cs of getting cited come in, namely: competence, collaboration, care, and communication. I'm not saying you should do any of these things just to get cited. That's a very instrumental approach that I would not encourage. But the four Cs are things you should do anyway as an academic. So, you might as well know that if you engage in them strategically, they will also increase your citations.

Competence

The first C stands for competence. Your work won't generally be cited if it isn't any good. If you've published terrible work, then it generally will not be cited. That is not always true, some very bad work does get cited and some very good work doesn't get cited. We can all find some of these counter examples. However, on average the better your work is, the more likely it will be cited. There is a match between the quality of your work and the level of citations it receives. Incidentally, the same is true for non-academic impact, which is typically based on rigorous research. In fact, the UK REF (Research Excellence Framework) requires the supporting research for REF external impact to be based on a certain level of publication quality.

Collaboration

Second, collaborate! Collaborate with other academics. Again, you are not doing that just to get more citations. There are many other reasons. First, it makes doing research much more fun. Working with academics who share your passion for a topic and who engage in a stimulating scholarly exchange is one of the most rewarding aspects of academia. Moreover, many co-authors become our academic friends too and we look forward to interacting with them.

Working with other people typically leads to better quality research too, because you generally collaborate with academics who have skills that are complementary to your own. You might be very good at theory development, but not so good at doing empirical research or vice versa. You might miss particular data analytical skills that a co-author might bring in.

I also find collaboration helps to iteratively improve and polish your paper, simply because you always have someone to read your paper critically. Of course, you can ask colleagues who are not co-authors to read the paper, but a co-author always has more motivation to read your paper critically than a colleague.

Finally, if you work with others on a project, there is more motivation to finish the project. You can tell yourself I'll just leave this paper, there are other more urgent things to do. But if you get emails in your inbox from your co-author saying: *"I've done my bit of the paper, you promised you would do your bit by ..."*, it's harder to say no than when you're just working on a paper on your own.

So, there are lots of intrinsic reasons to collaborate. However, another good reason is that co-authored papers generally tend to be cited much more than single authored papers. Again, this is not always true, there are always exceptions, but on average co-authored papers are cited much more. There are at least two reasons for that.

First, each of the authors has their own social network, so they can spread your co-authored article amongst their networks. Obviously, some of that network will overlap with yours, but some of it will be unique to your co-author. So, if you have three authors you might have at least twice the academic network. If you work in particle physics and have five hundred co-authors on a paper, then you might have 50 times the size of your own network. That makes a difference! It also shares the load in communicating about your paper.

Second, don't forget that your co-authors will generally cite you in other projects as well. This is partly because in doing so they're citing their own paper as well. But they are also simply more familiar with the work. In academia, you are not typically doing *all* your work with the same co-authors. So, these co-authors might well be working on related projects in which they are citing your co-authored paper.

——

The same collaboration benefit applies equally to societal impact. Collaboration with external stakeholders outside academia leads to better and more relevant research, but also to a better chance that the research will have impact.

Care

The third C stands for care. Care is important in general because it makes our profession a much nicer place to be. I feel very strongly about this. In fact, I made 2022 the year of positive academia and started writing LinkedIn recommendations for many dozens of my colleagues, mentees, co-authors, and other people I admire. More generally, however, I understand this concept of care in two ways, caring about your own reputation and caring for others.

Your reputation is your most valuable asset in academia. Nobody is keen to use or cite the work of an academic they don't respect. Academia is a *very* small world. If you are an early career researcher, you might not yet realise this, but academics *do* talk to each other about other academics. They even gossip, especially at conferences! We all know the academics who are what we call salami slicers; those who write up eight papers on one piece of research. We know the people who try to get their name on papers with others without doing any of the work. We know the academics that behave unethically. I go out of my way to avoid citing these people. There are always at least half a dozen papers you can cite to make a particular point. I'd rather cite someone who I know is a good and ethical researcher. So, care for your own reputation. Make sure that you don't ever engage in unethical behavior.

But also care for other academics and help them whenever you can. So, how does that work? First, do keep the promises you make at conferences. Do you recognise this? At a conference, you get talking about your shared research interests with another academic and say: *"I have some great resources on that. I have some papers and I'll send you that list"*. And then after the conference you come back home, and you don't do any of this. You get drawn back into your teaching and administration and you just forget. Or you might think that these people you met will probably forget about all these promises too.

That might well be true, but I don't think that's a sensible way to network or to make sure you create strong personal bonds. If I speak to people at conferences and I promise to do something, I ask for their business card and I write down what I promise to do. Then after the conference, I go through the business cards, and I just spent a few hours doing what I promised.

Something else I do regularly is to alert collaborators/colleagues/academic friends to useful information. If you read something that you think might be of interest to one of your mentees or co-authors, just send them a link or even the paper itself if you have it. It only takes a minute, but it might be a big help for someone else. Also, make sure you congratulate them on their achievements, especially if they are junior academics.

Then finally, and I can't stress this enough: *Thank* others for their help. If someone has spent time to help you, thank them. Over the years, I have help hundreds of academics with feedback on their papers or research ideas, responses to questions about academia, and thousands with technical support for Publish or Perish. Quite a lot of them can't seem to be bothered to even acknowledge my email, let alone say a few words of thanks. Sometimes I get a bit stroppy and resend the email after a few weeks and often get a *"yes, I was busy"* response, which leaves me thinking: *I took time out of my busy day to help you and you are too busy to take 2 minutes to thank me?* So please don't be that person, not with me and not with anyone else. If we do want academia to be a nicer place, we *all* need to play our role.

Communicate

Fourth and finally: communicate! It makes sense, doesn't it? People can't cite your work if they can't find it. So why do some academics make it so difficult to find their work? There are so many ways in which you can make your work available. Hence, I will devote a separate section to this.

How to communicate your research?

This section provides you with a very quick overview of what you can do to communicate your research. The next Chapter (Follow the 7 steps for impact) presents a step-by-step guide with practical examples of how to do this.

Create your own website

I have been running my own website since 1999 and it is the best thing I have ever done. You can put preprints of your papers online, provide an up-to-date list of publications, and provide a summary of your key research programs. Having a good online presence ensures that your papers are found easily if an academic searches for a topic relating to your research in Google.

For example, if you do a Google search with words relating to my own research interests my website generally features high up in the results. A search for "Language in international business" displays my research programme on this topic as the second result. The first result is an article derived from this research programme as featured on the publisher's website. Generic terms such as "journal quality" and "international survey research" also show up my website in the first 10 hits. You need a content rich website to achieve this, and you can't build this up in just a few years, so I recommend you start one early in your career.

Get your work listed in online repositories

Listing your work in online repositories is a good alternative to a personal website. It could be your own university repository, SSRN, arXiv, Academia.edu, or ResearchGate. There is no need to use all these services! Just pick one or two and make sure you keep them up to date. Remember if you don't do so, people might assume you haven't published anything for years...

At the very least ensure that you have a comprehensive Google Scholar Citation profile. Unless your name is very common, it only takes a few minutes to set up and it ensures that everyone can find an up-to-date list of your publications. This is even more important if you have a common name as most citation databases have poor author disambiguation (see also my blogpost *"Health warning: Might contain multiple personalities"*).

A very easy way to clean up a messy GSC profile is to use a Publish or Perish GSC profile search. By sorting the results in a variety of ways, which is impossible in GS itself, you can easily spot mistakes or inconsistencies that you can then fix in your profile. You can find more details see Chapter 6 and one of the other books in my Working in Academia series: *Creating social media profiles* (2023).

Attend conferences and network

Attend conferences, present your work, and *talk* to people. Don't just hang out with your friends. Volunteer to participate in, or even organise, Professional Development Workshops, act as a discussant or a session chair. This gives you the opportunity to introduce yourself to a dedicated and captive audience. Give them a few lines about your own research and impress the audience with your comments on the papers as well as your organisational skills. This is even more important for young academics that need to gain name recognition.

Use social media

Does this conference networking sound too hard for you? Are you a strong introvert (don't forget most academics are, they are just "playing extravert" for the duration of the conference)? Are you unable to travel for family or financial reasons? Or are you simply concerned about the environmental effects of conference travel. If so, becoming active on social media can be a good alternative.

Consider using Twitter to get relevant information in your field and tweet about any new research findings or publications. It does have its limitations, but I have picked a lot of useful information through Twitter that would have taken a much longer time through other sources. Tweeting about my white papers and blog posts increases their readership at least five or ten-fold, sometimes much more. That's not bad for a 280-character post! For some key tips on social media for academics, see Chapter 6 and my book on *Creating social media profiles* (2023).

Write up blog posts about your research. It can be enjoyable to write up your research findings in a format that is accessible to an audience larger than just your own "micro-tribe". If you have published a body of work on a certain topic, it can be a good way to distribute it more widely. For examples, see my blogposts *"To rank or not to rank"*, *"Challenges in International survey research: illustrations and solutions"*, *"What if fully agree doesn't mean the same thing across cultures?*, and *"Trailblazers of diversity: editors and editorial board diversity"*.

Don't think you need to be a senior academic to write blogposts. One of my co-authors – Helene Tenzer – wrote a guest post on my website about her research on managing multi-lingual teams when she was still quite junior. She then used this post to approach companies for a new research project as it gave them an accessible summary of her work. This works much better than sending them long emails or – horror of horrors – actual journal articles. Hence, blogposts do not only help to communicate your research to other academics, but they also excel at communicating with a non-academic audience.

Communicate by email

Finally, there is nothing wrong with using the "old-fashioned" way of communicating by email. Reading an unusually interesting paper in your own field? Email the author to tell them what you liked about it and send them one or two of your own *related* papers. Don't be shy to send your own papers; most academics appreciate it. It is hard for everyone to keep up to date. Do make sure you don't spam people though. For details, see Chapter 6 and my blogpost *"Don't write mass emails (1): distributing your work"*.

Isn't this unfair?

And if all of this sounds "unfair" to you and makes you think *"but surely if my work is good academics should just read and cite it"* and *"why should publicity and name recognition be needed"*, I can only agree. But gone are the days that academics had both the time and ability to keep up with all the good work in their field. Most academics have a pressured existence, and the volume of publications is rising ever more rapidly. Publicity, and brand recognition are crucial in almost any area of life these days, and I am afraid academia is no exception. Yes, most academics will still appreciate and recognise substance over packaging, but why not make it easier for them to appreciate the substance of your work!

In sum

In this chapter we reviewed the four Cs of getting cited: competence, collaboration, care, and communication. The next chapter will focus on the communication aspect. I will provide you with a step-by-step guide that allows you to maximise the chances your paper gets the impact it deserves by making it widely available and bringing it to the attention of your intended audience.

Chapter 6: Follow the 7 steps for impact

In Chapter 5 we talked about communication being one of the four Cs of getting cited. In this chapter we will discuss a practical, step by step process to communicate your newly accepted paper to the right audience. Although most of the seven steps are targeted at academic impact, measured by citations, the steps related to sharing the news about your paper on social media can certainly be a way to facilitate non-academic impact too.

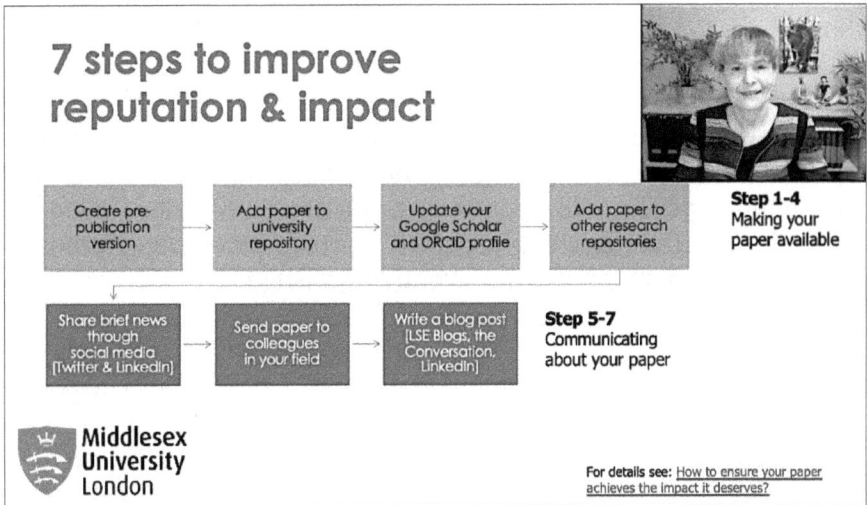

The first four steps in the process are all about making your paper available online to ensure it *can* be found by people who want to find it. The next three steps of the process involve communicating about your paper to increase the likelihood that people *will* find it. The above screenshot is from my recorded presentation on this topic and shows a summary of the seven steps. If you want to watch the video, go to my YouTube channel Harzing Academic Resources, or simply search for "7 steps for impact" on YouTube.

Step 1: Create a pre-publication version

As soon your paper is accepted for a journal, create a pre-publication version. So, what's a pre-publication version? It's basically the paper that was accepted for the journal, but not in the journal formatting. Nearly all publishers allow you to share a pre-publication version on the various social media platforms. However, even though a pre-publication version is not in the nice journal formatting, this doesn't mean you have to use the same manuscript you submitted to the journal. The latter tends to be double spaced with wide margins, with all the tables and features at the end. It doesn't look very attractive, nor is it easy to read.

So, what I do is I take the paper and change it from double spaced to 1.5 or single spaced. I ensure that there is a neat heading structure that I like, not the one that a journal requires. And I put all the tables and figures within the main body of the paper so readers can look at them whilst they are reading it. You can do any other things that make the paper look like something you can be proud of, even if it doesn't have the more sophisticated journal formatting. Here is an example for a paper that was recently published.

Blogpost: Turning ethnic similarity traps into social advantages

Whenever I have a paper accepted, I also put the abstract and a link to the pre-publication version itself on my website in the section online papers (see below). Once published, I then add the publication details. So, whenever someone wants to download any of my papers they can just go to this list. You might have your own website, for instance on Google Sites, where you can do this too. But if you don't you can always use paper repositories (see step 2 and 4).

Cultures and Institutions:
Dispositional and contextual explanations for country-of-origin effects in MNC "ethnocentric" staffing practices

Download paper (355 KB) - Publication details - Related blog post

February 2021 - Although the country-of-origin effect on staffing practices of multinational corporations (MNCs) is well-known, its underlying mechanisms are under-theorized. Drawing on the cross-cultural management and comparative institutionalism literatures, we propose an overarching, theory-based framework with two mechanisms, dispositional and contextual, that might explain country-of-origin effects in MNCs' use of parent-country nationals (PCNs) in their foreign subsidiaries' top management teams. The tendency of MNCs from some home countries to staff these positions with PCNs is typically labeled as "ethnocentric", a word imbued with negative intentions referring mainly to the dispositional rationale behind this staffing choice. However, fuzzy-set qualitative comparative analysis (fsQCA) of staffing practices of MNCs from ten home countries shows that both mechanisms – dispositional and contextual – have considerable explanatory power. Our methodological approach enables us to analyze conceptually distinct, yet empirically intertwined, societal-level explanations as a pattern, and thus offers a viable solution to integrate different perspectives in international and comparative research.

2020

The double-edged sword of ethnic similarity for expatriates

Download paper (271KB) - Publication details - Related blog post

October 2020 - Identifying employees to represent headquarters (HQ) effectively in overseas units is a management challenge faced by all multinational corporations (MNCs). To date, management of this type of expatriate employees has accorded a central role to culture, such as understanding cultural differences, facilitating cultural adaptation and adjustment, and cultivating cultural intelligence. Although culture is a critical factor in explaining expatriates' experiences, identity offers an alternative angle to reveal the challenges that occur when expatriates interact with host country employees. In this article, we introduce ethnically similar expatriates – a sub-category of expatriates who share an ethnicity with host country employees – to showcase the role of identity, especially the interpersonal dynamics associated with ethnic similarity.

Step 2: Add paper to university repository

For many academics the first step after creating the pre-publication version is to deposit this paper in your University's paper repository. In the UK this needs to be done within three months of *acceptance*. This is compulsory. If you don't, it doesn't count for the REF (the UK's national research evaluation). That means your university is losing out, both in terms of REF ranking and in terms of research funding. Ultimately, this means you will lose out too. So, whenever you have a paper accepted, make sure the first thing you do is depositing it into your University repository.

Step 3: Update your Google Scholar and ORCID profiles

The next step is updating your key researcher profiles. There are many different research profiles, but the most important profiles are arguably your university's staff profile, your Google Scholar profile and your ORCID profile. Most university staff profiles have a link to your university's repository and draw in publications automatically. So, there is no need to do anything there.

Most university repositories are also covered by Google Scholar, which normally picks up any new additions to repositories within a few days, certainly within a week. This means that once your paper is in your University's repository, everyone can find it on Google Scholar. This is particularly important for book chapters which are hard to find through other means.

You can also update your ORCID profile at this stage, but ORCID is usually a bit slower to find your paper online, so you might need to enter it manually. Hence, you may want to wait a few more weeks until ORCID discovers it through one of its automatic feeds or until the paper is published with a DOI in online first. Below you can see the various options for adding your article to your ORCID profile.

Google Scholar capturing repository items

To show how seamless the process of interaction between Google Scholar and your university repository is, here is a book chapter I recently published with one of my former PhD students in an edited book. As I mentioned above, public access is even more important for book chapters, as they are difficult to find through other means.

So, I included a pre-publication version of this book chapter in the Middlesex University repository (see above). As you can see from the image below, the repository entry was captured in Google Scholar. The indication in the top right hand corner shows that Google Scholar knows a PDF of the chapter can be found in the MDX repository.

It only took a few days for the repository entry to appear on Google Scholar. If you have a Google Scholar profile, Google will even send you an email saying they have found a new paper for you. As you can see below the Google Scholar entry lists the full abstract.

The hyperlinked title links to the publisher's version of the chapter, in this case Emerald Publishing. So, anyone working at a university with a subscription to Emerald's books can also read the official publisher's version.

By Mutual Agreement: How Can Ethnically Similar Expatriates Engage Host Country Employees *

Shea X. Fan, Anne-Wil Harzing
Intercultural Management in Practice
ISBN: 978-1-83982-827-0, eISBN:
978-1-83982-826-3
Publication date: 16 August 2021

Step 4: Add paper to research repositories

Step 4 involves putting your paper in a public repository, where the level of engagement with other academics will likely be higher than in your university repository. There are a lot of different options. First there are general repositories such as SSRN and ArXiv, which were established decades ago. Initially these were mainly used by Natural and Life Scientists, but increasingly academics in other disciplines find them useful too. Make sure you talk to your colleagues to find out what they are using. It doesn't make sense to deposit your paper in a repository that nobody in your discipline uses. Colleagues are not going to look for your paper there.

In the past decade, a different kind of repositories emerged, such as ResearchGate or Academia.edu. They are more like social media platforms for academics. I don't use Academia.edu, but I do have a ResearchGate account. The process for adding papers is blissfully simple. ResearchGate usually discovers your paper online and when you log in it will have a recommendation to add that paper to your account with a few clicks. Depending on your settings, you might even get an email reminder doing this. Then all you need to do is add the full-text version, which you have already prepared in step 1.

Below are a few examples of public repositories. First, arXiv where one of my co-authors in Computer Science regularly deposits their papers. Second, SSRN where many of our Economist colleagues post their papers. I have shown a few papers by Praveen Kujal, the head of our Economics department.

Computer Science > Digital Libraries

[Submitted on 27 Apr 2018]

Can we use Google Scholar to identify highly-cited documents?

Alberto Martín-Martín, Enrique Orduna-Malea, Anne-Wil Harzing, Emilio Delgado López-Cózar

The main objective of this paper is to empirically test whether the identification of highly-cited documents through Google Scholar is feasible and reliable. To this end, we carried out a longitudinal analysis (1950 to 2013), running a generic query (filtered only by year of publication) to minimise the effects of academic search engine optimisation. This gave us a final sample of 64,000 documents (1,000 per year). The strong correlation between a document's citations and its position in the search results (r= -0.67) led us to conclude that Google Scholar is able to identify highly-cited papers effectively. This, combined with Google Scholar's unique coverage (no restrictions on document type and source), makes the academic search engine an invaluable tool for bibliometric research relating to the identification of the most influential scientific documents. We find evidence, however, that Google Scholar ranks those documents whose language (or geographical web domain) matches with the user's interface language higher than could be expected based on citations. Nonetheless, this language effect and other factors related to the Google Scholar's operation, i.e. the proper identification of versions and the date of publication, only have an incidental impact. They do not compromise the ability of Google Scholar to identify the highly-cited papers.

Download:
• PDF only
(license)

Current browse context:
cs.DL
< prev | next >
new | recent | 1804
Change to browse by:
cs

References & Citations
• NASA ADS
• Google Scholar
• Semantic Scholar

DBLP – CS Bibliography
listing | bibtex

Alberto Martín-Martín
Enrique Orduña-Malea
Anne-Wil Harzing
Emilio Delgado López-Cózar

Export Bibtex Citation

Bookmark

SSRN

Product & Services   Subscribe   Submit a paper   Browse   Rankings   Contact   Create acc

You searched: praveen kujal   Search Within

Sort by: Date Posted, Descending

Viewing: 1 - 18 of 18 papers

1. Mixture and Distribution of Different Water Qualities: An Experiment on Alternative Scenarios Concerning Vertical Structure in a Complex Market
LINEEX Working Paper No. 12/00
Number of pages: 56 · Posted: 06 Feb 2001
Nikolaos Georgantzis, Nikolaos Georgantzis, Aurora Garcia-Gallego, Enrique Fatas, Praveen Kujal and Tibor Neugebauer
LINEEX and University Jaume I of Castellón, Laboratori d'Economia Experimental (LEE), Universitat Jaume I, University of East Anglia (UEA) - Centre for Behavioural and Experimental Social Science (CBESS), Universidad Carlos III de Madrid - Department of Economics and University of York - Derwent College
Keywords: Water Management, Experimental Economics, Vertical Structure

Downloads 127

2. International Trade Policy towards Monopoly and Oligopoly
Banco de España Working Paper No. 0901
Number of pages: 27 · Posted: 20 Feb 2009
Praveen Kujal and Juan M. Ruiz
Universidad Carlos III de Madrid - Department of Economics and Banco de España - Department of International Economics
Keywords: product differentiation, strategic trade policy, policy reversals, R&d subsidies, monopoly, duopoly

Downloads 77

3. The Relative Efficacy of Price Announcements and Express Communication for Collusion: Experimental Findings
Number of pages: 44 · Posted: 26 Nov 2014
Joseph E. Harrington Jr, Roberto Hernan Gonzalez and Praveen Kujal

Downloads 74

Third, Academia.edu which is used quite a lot by academics in the Humanities. I included the profile of my colleague Nico Pizzolato who is a historian. Finally, one of my own papers on ResearchGate, where you can see it is available in full text.

There is a lot more you can do with ResearchGate, you can create research projects, submit questions, answer other people's questions, and check out your statistics for reads and citations. If you are interested in learning more have a look at my blogpost *"Social media in Academia (5): ResearchGate"* or read my book on *Creating social media profiles* (2023).

Step 5: Share news through social media

With your paper available on all the relevant platforms, the next step is to start communicating about it. First, write up a short blogpost about your new paper. Just write a few lines to introduce the paper, include the full paper reference and the abstract, link to the full-text version and that's it. You can then share it through social media. I mainly use Twitter and LinkedIn, but you can use any platform.

If you don't have your own website or blog, LinkedIn is a perfect alternative. You can post updates of your own work, either through short posts or through full-blown articles. This is a good way to start distributing your work as you already have a ready-made audience on LinkedIn through your connections. And if you don't want to go through the effort of writing up something, you can also just take a screenshot of the abstract and share that on Twitter or LinkedIn.

Below is a slide from my recorded presentation on research impact with an example. This is the article I mentioned in step 1. It was first authored by my former PhD student Shea Fan. I wrote up a short blogpost on the paper. It introduced Shea's work and mentioned our positive experience with the journal in which the article was published. Just think of anything that makes the post a bit more personal. Then choose an evocative image to go with the post and you are all ready to go (see left-hand image).

I then shared this blogpost on LinkedIn with the sharing button on my website (see middle image). If you don't have your own website, just write directly on LinkedIn. Subsequently, Shea tweeted about it (see right-hand image). If you look very closely, you can see that she also included a separate link to ResearchGate so that people could immediately download the pre-publication version there.

Remember that you can share your paper multiple times. I wouldn't recommend you doing so several times a week, but it is perfectly fine to share it half a dozen times a year. People are not glued to social media. Well, at least I hope not. Any single communication will therefore only reach a small number of people. So, unlike academic articles, republishing blogposts is perfectly fine.

Step 6: Sending a personal email

In the age or social media, email might seem a bit "old-fashioned", but it is still a very important means of communication for academics in my generation. Many academics in this age group will not be heavy social media users. So, they might not even see any of your messages on these platforms. Yet, they might be and important audience, as they typically hold positions of influence.

You might have published a paper and think "*it would be really great if that (senior) person would read my work, because I have drawn on their work in my research, I've met this person at a number of conferences*". But you can't be sure they would pick up the article if you didn't point it out to them. Or they might pick it up, but only in a year's time when it appears in print. A personal email works wonders.

So, make it easy to send out these emails to other academics. I keep all my papers in a folder in my computer. If anyone sends me an email saying that they are interested in a one of my papers, it takes me literally less than a minute to send the response back. If it's someone I know well or would like to engage with I'll write a slightly longer email but otherwise it's just a quick email with "*Thank you for your interest in my work, please find the paper you requested attached. Hope you enjoy reading it*".

But as I said, you can also do this *proactively*. It really is a good way to start building up your network, especially if you are a junior academic. At the same time, you don't want to be obnoxious. So, don't send one and the same email to a whole group of people all in bcc (let alone in the "to" field).

Don't do mass mailings, it's email clutter at best and spamming at worst and won't build a positive academic identity. Also, make sure it is a nice email. So, don't write the equivalent of: *"here's my very important paper, now go and read it"*. Write a nice introduction like: *"you might not remember me, but we met at…, and I thought you might be interested in this paper, because…"*.

Here is an example of an effective email communications. It is an email I received a while ago from a PhD student whom I met when I gave a presentation at Victoria university in New Zealand. She had now finished her PhD, and published a couple of articles, one of which she featured in her email. What she also did was include a picture of herself. I normally don't expect people to do this, but in this case, it was quite useful because it had been it had been 7 or 8 years since I saw her.

An effective communication: example 1

Here is what I think was a particularly good example: personal, courteous, interesting, and introducing something I hadn't heard about before: a doodle research illustration. The picture was useful too as I had not met this student for 8 years.

> I don't know if you remember me, but I met you at Victoria University (NZ) when you came to speak many years ago. At the time I was a PhD student researching multilingualism and the role of English in banks in Luxembourg.
>
> Now, I'm delighted to share with you what I have just published on YouTube. It's a short 20 minute illustration (doodle) on some aspects of my PhD. It's a video that could be used as a teaching resource. I've attached a free e-print from the 2013 journal article that goes with. I hope you enjoy it as much as I did in producing it!

https://www.youtube.com/watch?v=1O1yE9ylqZo

http://www.tandfonline.com/eprint/VQn6deUXGpAkvGBDDgr7/full

Best wishes,
Leilarna Kingsley, *[Picture included]*

She had also created a Doodle about her research, a video with live hand-drawn animations which build up a story about your research. I thought it was a neat way to summarise the paper's key messages in a really engaging way. As this was something new for me as well, I was keen to have a look. As you can see the Doodle has had more than 2,500 views to date, so it did create quite a bit of exposure for the paper.

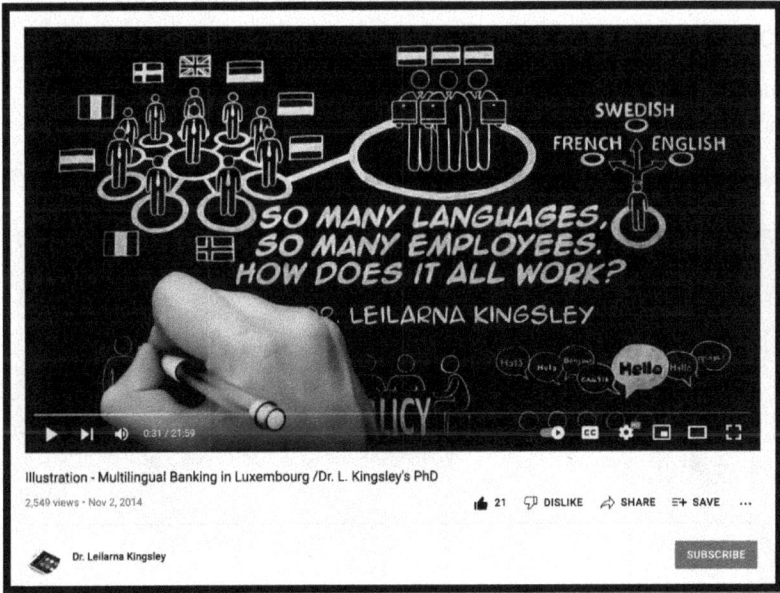

SWEDISH
FRENCH ENGLISH

SO MANY LANGUAGES,
SO MANY EMPLOYEES.
HOW DOES IT ALL WORK?

LEILARNA KINGSLEY

Hello

▶ ▶| ◄») 0:31 / 21:59   ►● CC ⚙ ▣ ▭ ⛶

Illustration - Multilingual Banking in Luxembourg /Dr. L. Kingsley's PhD

2,549 views · Nov 2, 2014   👍 21   👎 DISLIKE   ↪ SHARE   ☰+ SAVE   ...

Dr. Leilarna Kingsley   SUBSCRIBE

Step 7: Write up full blogpost on your paper

Step 7 is by far the most time-consuming step of the whole process, writing up a full-length blogpost about your paper. This is different from the Step 5 "abstract + a few lines" blogpost. Blogging is something you can do pretty much on any topic. I blog on my own website on a range of academic skills, the Publish or Perish software, academic etiquette, and the CYGNA women's network. However, I also write about my own research, and that's what this step is about.

You can write up a blogpost about an individual article. Below is an example of a guest post by my co-author Hyun-Jung Lee about our 2022 article in Organization Studies: *Cultures and Institutions: Dispositional and contextual explanations for country-of-origin effects in MNC "ethnocentric" staffing practices.* Hyun-Jung outlined the paper's key contributions in simple terms. Here are the first few lines.

Beyond ethnocentrism: why do MNCs send their nationals to subsdiaries?

Reframing our perspectives on "ethnocentric" staffing: a new article in Organization Studies

Hyun-Jung Lee - Thu 2 Dec 2021 14:20 (updated Thu 2 Jun 2022 11:54)

Why do MNCs send parent country nationals (PCNs) to staff top-management teams in their foreign subsidiaries? This is a classic research topic in international business and human resource management. Many studies have indicated that subsidiary's top-management staffing practices differ by the MNCs' country of origin (COO). The predominant explanation for such differences has been the "ethnocentric" culture of the MNC home country. Thus such practice is usually labelled as "ethnocentric" staffing.

A few months earlier, our co-author for this paper, Katsu Yoshikawa, had already written the "abstract and a few introductory lines" blogpost, but this was a proper post outlining the key arguments of our paper and how they contributed to the wider scholarly debate.

A few months later, during a recorded interview, I was asked about my recent research, and I mentioned this paper. This led to a neat 1-minute video in which I outlined the key message of our paper. This provided us with three different communication options from the three co-authors, providing us with an excellent base to diffuse our work through the various social media.

In addition to writing up a blogpost about an individual article, you can also write up an integrative post about several of your articles. Remember, you don't generally create research impact by publishing *one* article on a particular topic; you create research impact by having a research *stream* on a particular topic. Thus, it makes sense to collate articles on a similar theme in one substantive blogpost. This is also an excellent way to "revitalise" interest in older publications as you can show how they build up to your more recent work.

On the next page you can see an example of a blogpost that reviews a body of work on international survey research. In addition to discussing each of the three articles I published on this topic (the 3rd being visible in the image), I also included a selection of articles on methodological issues published in *Journal of International Business Studies*. As such, the post was intended to be useful reading for any scholars doing survey research in international business.

Challenges in International survey research: illustrations and solutions

Reviews my work on international mail surveys and response rates across countries

Anne-Wil Harzing - Mon 3 Apr 2017 17:08 (updated Fri 19 Aug 2022 12:47)

Putting it all together

In 2013, Sebastian Reiche, Markus Pudelko and I pulled together our experience in international survey research and provided a comprehensive and practical review in a paper published in the *European Journal of International Management*. We discussed every stage of the research process, including defining the study population, gaining data access, survey development, data collection, data analysis, and finally publication of the results.

For each stage, we review the pertinent literature, provide illustrations based on examples from our own research projects, and offer possible solutions to address the inherent challenges by formulating suggestions for improving the quality of international survey research. As EJIM's proactive editor – Vlad Vaiman ⬚ – realised the importance of making this paper widely accessible, it is available for free at the EJIM website ⬚.

References

- Harzing, A.W. (1997) **Response rates in international mail surveys: Results of a 22 country study**, *International Business Review*, 6(6): 641-665. Available online... - Publisher's version ⬚
- Harzing, A.W. (2000) **Cross-national industrial mail surveys: Why do response rates differ between countries**, *Industrial Marketing Management*, 29(3): 243-254. Available online... - Publisher's version ⬚
- Harzing, A.W.; Reiche B.S.; Pudelko, M. (2013) **Challenges in international survey research: A review with illustrations and suggested solutions for best practice**, *European Journal of International Management*, 7(1): 112-134. Available online... - Publisher's version ⬚ (free access!)

Blogging platforms

There are a lot of different outlets for blogposts. You can start your own blog. There are plenty of platforms out there that allow you to do this, such as WordPress or Blogger. But that's a big commitment. You can also start small by posting on Medium, which is a collective platform in which you have your "own corner". But on these general platforms you might see your blogposts drown in a sea of lifestyle blogposts.

Therefore, if you don't have an established academic profile yet, you are much better off writing for an established academic blog. First, check whether your university has its own blogging platform. Middlesex runs the MDX Minds blog (see the top left screenshot on the next page). Posting on your university's blog promotes not only your own research, but also your university. So, it will make your Head of Department and Dean happy too! Very few academics are active bloggers. This means that your university will typically be keen to accept your blogpost to keep their blogging platform active.

If you work in the Social Sciences, you can also try the LSE Blogs. LSE has 60 different blogs, including LSE Business Review, British and European Politics & Policy, Behavioural Science, Equality Diversity & Inclusion, Social Policy, and International Development. Some of the posts on my own blog were reprinted on the LSE Impact of the Social Sciences blog (see the posts on Google Scholar and citation metrics below). Another option is the Conversation (see the post on blockchain and musicians) which posts news stories and commentaries that are based on research. It is well-respected, and journalists increasingly use if for accessible summaries of research which they then write about in the more traditional newspapers. This creates a multiplier effect for your research.

If external blogs are not an option, because your research doesn't fit or you'd like to get something out quickly, you can also just write up an article on LinkedIn. Doing a series of these will allow you to build up a profile there. My Business School colleague Nico Pizzolato (see three posts on the right) has published a dozen articles on topics around academic writing and research skills, which fits very well with his role as Director of Doctorate Programs.

In sum

With just seven easy steps you can maximise the chance that your newly accepted paper finds the right audience. This process might all seem like too much work to you. But honestly, it isn't as time-consuming as you may think. Per paper this would take you about six to sixteen hours. That may still sound like quite a lot to you for a single paper. But please put this into context: you've spent years on this research and then another year or two writing up the paper and getting it through the review process. Why wouldn't you spend just one or two more days to make sure that your paper reaches the right audience?

Chapter 7: Research process versus research outcome

So far, our discussion has mainly focused on research *outputs*. I would argue, however, that in the production of impactful research, the research *process* is as important as the resource *outcome*. Yes, it is important that we contribute to the scholarly discourse. Of course, we would like our research to have societal impact through addressing some of the most pressing problems of our times such as climate change, growing inequality, or migration. However, this also needs to be coupled with an impactful research *process* that is supportive, inclusive, and collaborative, and conducts research with integrity.

Producing impactful research *outcomes* is all well and good. But what if the underlying research *process* involved questionable research practices or even outright research misconduct? What if these outcomes were achieved through exploitation of a precarious workforce? What if junior collaborators were not given due recognition? Even without actively engaging in these dubious research practices, academics might achieve impactful research *outcomes* by focusing purely on their own research, neglecting the many other academic roles that are essential to our profession. This includes the many "discretionary" service activities such as engaging in peer review, mentoring junior academics, writing references, and more generally creating positive academic cultures. So, in this chapter we will discuss what an impactful research process might look like.

What is an impactful research process?

It is hard to measure these less "tangible" or "visible" aspects making up an impactful research *process*. This is where a movement such as the Humane Metrics Initiative comes in. Although focused on the Humanities, I would argue that their five key values are applicable to all disciplines. Below left are its five key values, values that also underlie my work at Middlesex university (below right).

HuMetrics explicitly focuses on the research process rather than only the research outcome. Their website encourages us to:

> Re-examine how we think about scholarly work, moving away from a "product"-oriented mentality and toward a "process"-oriented one. It is one of our core beliefs that doing, recognizing, and rewarding scholarly activity that is rooted in our values makes for a better academy. It can be hard to think about what values-inflected scholarship might look like when you focus on the object alone rather than the processes that went into it. Focusing on the processes, though, gives us space to enact our values through micro-transactional decisions, to shift from the "what" to the "how": how the sausage is made, not just on the sausage.

Of their five values, the values of openness and soundness are more directly related to the research process, whereas equity, collegiality, and community relate to how academics interact with each other and the world outside academia. Inevitably, some of these values will overlap. For instance, it is hard to determine where collegiality ends, and community building begins. Moreover, each of the five values connects with the others. For instance, a focus on openness makes certain aspects of soundness easier to achieve. However, below we will discuss each of these individual values in a bit more detail.

Equity

In its external orientation, this value relates mostly to a willingness to undertake studies with social justice, equitable access to research, and the public good in mind. It has significant overlap with calls to focus our research on "Grand Challenges" and doing research with societal impact, which is now a commonplace goal at many universities. Middlesex University's purpose is *"to create knowledge and put it into action to develop fairer, healthier, more prosperous, and sustainable societies"*, whereas its vision is *"to transform outcomes for individuals, communities and organisations and to empower people to change their lives"*. Middlesex University Business School was ranked first in the United Kingdom for societal impact in the 2021 national research evaluation (see Chapter 1).

However, even fields that can be seen as more managerial do lend themselves to research topics that meet the value of equity. Below is an example in one of my own research fields: global mobility. The slide reviews some of the Grand Challenges and how mobility research can contribute. It is part of a presentation *"Dare to be different, why IHRM research needs to change"* which also discussed the need to broaden our population, to improve our theoretical grounding, to use novel research methods, and to take interdisciplinarity seriously. Finally, it encouraged researchers to dare to be different and critical.

Equity in the world of academia

We also need to apply equity to academia itself by ensuring that all voices are heard and that our university and research cultures are inclusive. The below slide is part of a presentation that I gave for the European Foundation for Management Development (EFMD) on *"Supporting ECAs & MCAs with collaborative & inclusive cultures"*.

In this presentation, I discussed how most new recruits in universities in general, and Business Schools in particular, are academics from "non-majority groups", i.e., they are non-local, female, and non-native speakers of the local language. This is particularly the case for universities in Anglophone countries. At Middlesex University for instance less than 20% of our academic staff are from a white Anglo background, and three quarters of these are over 60 years old.

Research shows that female and international academics often do not feel included in the dominant culture. They also face higher barriers in progression and promotion. Hence, universities need to urgently match their strategic rhetoric of equality, diversity, and inclusion with on the ground day-to-day practice that clearly evidence their appreciation of a variety of backgrounds and perspectives. They need to understand that effective and efficient collaboration requires *reciprocal* adjustments, rather than a focus on integrating "minority groups" into the dominant culture.

Openness

Openness has strong parallels with the Open Science movement, which advocates making scientific research (including publications, data, physical samples, and software) accessible to all levels of society, amateur or professional. Although this is a movement that I am strongly supportive of, I haven't been at the forefront of this. So, I will refrain from discussing this in any detail and instead refer you to the excellent website of the Center for Open Science (cos.io).

Collegiality

With its composite values of empathy, respect, kindness, generosity, and self-care, HuMetrics third value is one that is very close to my heart. Most of my work in mentoring junior academics at Middlesex and in leading the CYGNA women's network is based on exactly these values. I was even awarded a Leading Lights "Kindness in leadership" award in 2019 and received the inaugural Positive Leadership award in 2023, as one of only 24 out of nearly 12,000 nominees.

It is encouraging that many academic institutions are now starting to explicitly recognise the importance of collegiality in their promotion guidelines. Although collegiality is essential for the smooth functioning of *any* organisation, as well as for the well-being of its employees, promotion guidelines in most universities still emphasise individual achievements and reinforce competition.

In 2022 Middlesex University completely revamped its promotion criteria. The new criteria make collegiality an explicit element of any application.

> *Collegiality is seen as a key factor in ensuring the successful implementation of the Strategy and so it is a core criterion for promotion. All candidates must explicitly demonstrate how they have upheld the principles of the University and provide evidence of how they contribute to the delivery of the University Strategy.*

The guidelines suggest that evidencing good academic citizenship can take many forms and includes:

- Contributing to an inclusive community through promoting equality and diversity.

- Supporting the career development of colleagues, including mentoring, support, peer review and relevant collaborations, particularly in relation to early career colleagues.

- Voluntary or civic engagement activities in line with the University's strategic goals.

- Taking on Departmental, Faculty or University roles which may be over and above what may be expected.

Supporting early and mid-career academics

For me a crucial aspect of collegiality is a focus on supporting early and mid-career academics. It may sound trite, but they really *are* the future. They also have a larger stake in the future. Their attitudes are a good fit with today's world (see the slide of my EFMD presentation below). Most young academics I meet are incredibly passionate about doing research with real societal significance. Not having experienced as many setbacks and rejections, they also still have their youthful enthusiasm. Junior scholars are also more likely to have the skill set that suits today's *academic* world. They are more likely to be eager to engage with social media and Open Science and are less fixated on standard career paths.

The Core 3:
Focus on ECAs and MCAs

- Junior scholars' attitudes fit today's world
  - Passionate to do research with real societal significance
  - Enthusiastic, not cynical/jaded like many of our generation ☺
- Junior scholars' skills fit today's academic world
  - Engaging externally through social media
  - Being committed to Open Science
  - Expecting a variety of career paths
- What is the role of senior scholars?
  - Public intellectuals, policy-making, academic service, supporting ECAs and MCAs
  - Balancing act: smooth their paths through wisdom, building connections, but let them choose their own routes

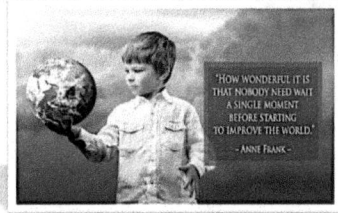

Middlesex
University
London

"HOW WONDERFUL IT IS
THAT NOBODY NEED WAIT
A SINGLE MOMENT
BEFORE STARTING
TO IMPROVE THE WORLD."
— ANNE FRANK —

So, what is the role of senior scholars in all of this? I strongly believe that senior scholars should focus on giving back. Some are naturally suited to be public intellectuals. Some get heavily involved in policy-making or academic service activities. But we need many to take on the role of supporting junior academics, especially as their employment conditions are often more precarious than those of previous generations.

Self-care

The HuMetrics value of collegiality also includes self-care. Although I do not share the negative view of some of my senior colleagues (see my YouTube video: "*Why academia can still be a great career*"), I am the first to acknowledge that an academic career can be very demanding, not least because our work is such an important part of our identity. Hence, we often end up working long hours, which is not sustainable over the course of a career. Self-care is thus crucial.

For a more in-depth perspective, I can highly recommend Martina Śliwa's presentation (see below) that shows how important it is to consider career development planning in the context of personal wellbeing and sustainability. It combines a refreshing dose of realism with a review of the common challenges faced, and some excellent strategies and tactics for building a career in a sustainable way.

How to create a sustainable academic career

Reports on Martyna Sliwa's presentation on career progression in the UK higher education environment

Anne-Wil Harzing - Sat 21 Nov 2020 14:35 (updated Sun 21 Aug 2022 09:27)

'How to build a sustainable academic career'

Prof. Martyna Śliwa,
Essex Business School

Watch on ▶ YouTube

My current academic passions are creating a better understanding of the role of language in IB (and academia), improving research evaluation in the Social Sciences, and helping academics find their way in an increasingly competitive academic world. It is therefore not surprising that I am a big fan of Martyna Śliwa's ⧉ work which touches upon many of these themes, sometimes even in one and the same project (see also: On academic life: collaborations and active engagement ⧉).

Soundness

This value complements openness with its focus on reproducibility and integrity, both facilitated by Open Science. It also emphasises originality, creativity, boundary pushing, and knowledge advancement, in contrast to practising safe and incremental research. I made similar arguments in one of my webinars entitled *"Dare to be different, why IHRM research needs to change"*, emphasising the importance of being different and critical. You can find this presentation on my YouTube channel: Harzing Academic Resources.

Be different

In this presentation, I talked about the double standards for what is seen as "valid" research. White male researchers from WEIRD (Western, Educated, Industrial, Rich, and Democratic) countries can study their own population without needing to provide any justification. Research with this population is seen as "universally valid". However, if a female ethnic Chinese researcher studies a female ethnic Chinese population, it is derogatively called _me_search.

Rather than seeing this as a problem, we _should_ encourage different researchers to study different populations. At the same time, we should leverage author collaborations across ethnic boundaries for a more holistic understanding; I have learned a huge amount from my collaborators worldwide. For instance, with one of my Chinese PhD students I had endless discussions about the relative importance of ethnicity versus nationality and culture across countries.

I am also a strong advocate of preserving creativity and originality by writing less formulaic papers. In fact, many of my more unusual papers, though hard to publish, ultimately had much more scholarly impact. Endorsing creativity and originality also includes writing for audiences beyond academia. Diffusing our research in practitioner journals and social media is an essential part of our job.

Be critical

I also feel very strongly about being critical (see below). Science is about progress. Just because an article was written by someone who now is a famous researcher doesn't mean it can't be improved upon. For instance, my 2001 article *Bears, bumblebees, and spiders: the role of expatriates in controlling foreign subsidiaries* contained very simplistic analyses. I came up with the metaphors in a light-hearted discussion with my husband. So, I was quite shocked to learn that some junior scholars now seem to regard the typology as gospel.

My first ever article – which I wrote as a PhD student – showed that the persistent myth of high expatriate failure rates was created by massive (mis)referencing. I was apprehensive about publishing it as it critiqued the work of so many senior academics in my field. But being critical is essential to advance scholarship. Just make sure you do it respectfully and with sufficient justification.

I have also learned to not give up on a topic that you feel strongly about, even if your argument is not fully accepted the first time. I followed up my 1995 article on academic myth creation with a second article that generalised it, providing twelve guidelines for good academic referencing. It drew broader conclusions about the impact of inaccurate referencing on academia, practice, and the interaction between the two and is now featured on many PhD syllabi.

Early in my career I also published an article that was provocatively subtitled *"From neglect to myopia?"*. I argued that sample idiosyncrasies and a focus on secondary data, coupled with blind confidence in a specific measurement of cultural distance, led researchers to overestimate its role in entry mode decisions. Published in a book rather than a journal, the piece was largely ignored. However, a follow-up in 2016 *"Do we need to distance ourselves from the distance concept"* that contained empirical research became a very highly cited article.

So, keep practicing the value of soundness: don't give up, be original, be creative, and keep pushing those boundaries. Collectively we can advance knowledge.

Community

The fifth and final value of the HuMetrics initiative is a bit fuzzier. For me it links strongly with both collegiality and equity. However, the HuMetrics website lists several aspects of the value of community that are worthwhile to explore a bit further: relationships and networks, the role of senior academics, and digital preservation.

Relationships and networks

HuMetrics see relationships and networks as crucial to community in scholarly life (see quote). An important aspect of this is a focus on *reciprocity*, a culture where early, mid, and late career researchers learn from each other, rather than seeing senior academics as the fountain of wisdom. Junior academics are often more up to date with methodological innovations, Open Science, and using social media.

> *Paying attention to community in scholarly life means fostering, cultivating, and participating in relationships and networks to which one gives and from which one takes. Like collegiality, it's about generosity and mentorship; it's about knowing when to lead and when to listen.*

So how would this work in practice? Here are two examples from my own work at Middlesex University.

Staff development groups

One of the first initiatives I set up after joining Middlesex University in 2014 were regular staff development group meetings. They were informal 2-hour gatherings in which we discussed draft papers and research ideas, but also opened the floor to impromptu questions about anything related to academia. I typically ran 3-5 streams every 6 weeks, with 4-6 academics in each group. As group composition varied, they also had a strong community building element. Academics got to know colleagues they had been working alongside for many years, but had never talked to.

What was crucial to these groups, however, was that participants would *receive* as well as *provide* advice and resources. Although I would always be there as an "advisor of last resort", most of the time my role was being a facilitator. Those participants that understood and appreciated the community element kept coming back. Others joined only when they needed feedback on their own work. No prizes for guessing who ultimately gained more from this initiative!

Positive academia

Another initiative that was squarely targeted at community building sprang from the 2nd pandemic Winter. With spirits being quite low, I decided to commit to making 2022 the year of Positive Academia. This doesn't mean I don't recognise the problems we are facing in academia; it simply means that I am committed to showing that there are positive sides too. So, in the Christmas holidays, I started writing LinkedIn recommendations for my colleagues, mentees, co-authors, and others I admire. I am currently at around 60 and am hoping to write many more.

Beyond simply putting a smile on your colleagues' face, LinkedIn recommendations are also useful for academics going up for tenure or promotion as they constitute public evidence. They are very useful in evidencing performance in leadership and collegiality where "objective" metrics are harder to find. However, they can be used for any aspect of an academic career. So please take this small step to support an academic colleague. I am sure they will be pleasantly surprised. If you'd like some tips on how to write recommendations, refer to the blogpost below.

Using LinkedIn recommendations to support others

Use the LinkedIn recommendation feature to write testimonials for people in your network

Anne-Wil Harzing - Mon 6 Jun 2022 08:25 (updated Tue 26 Jul 2022 17:58)

Academics are all familiar with writing references, whether it is for our students, our (former) colleagues, or for external tenure and promotion cases. But these long and carefully crafted letters are read only by a small number of people. Why not write a short recommendation on a public platform such as LinkedIn, where everyone can read it? In this post I show how to use LinkedIn's recommendation feature ⸬ to support other academics in your network.

Small acts of kindness can be part of your daily working life and don't have to take up a lot of your time. Reading a particularly well-crafted email about a difficult topic? Send the writer a quick note saying you appreciate how much work went into it and how much you like the result. This is crucial for junior academics who might agonise whether they struck the right tone. However, it is equally important for senior managers (e.g., Department Heads or Deans). Being in a senior position can be quite alienating and lonely.

Like a paper you read? Share it on LinkedIn or Twitter with your personal reflections. Send an appreciative email to an author whose work you enjoyed reading or to someone who has done a great job as an editor, as a conference organizer, or even as a panel chair. The possibilities are literally endless. For some examples to inspire you, see the blogpost below.

Changing academic culture: one email at a time...

Shows how we can all contribute to making academia a nicer and kinder place to be

Anne-Wil Harzing - Sun 6 Jun 2021 05:54 (updated Sun 21 Aug 2022 09:08)

I am sure you have heard it all before. Academia is too competitive. We focus too much on the spectacular successes, ignoring more mundane, but essential activities. Academic stars are often held up as hero role models, even though teamwork is essential. We can't change academic cultures overnight. But what if I told you that we **can** all take little steps to make academia a kinder place, one email or social media post at a time...

The role of senior academics

In the previous section I mentioned that everyone can play a role in building a positive academic community. Even so, senior academics carry an additional responsibility. Many senior academics are constantly complaining about the "state of academia". However, this complaining often takes the form of publications in top journals and simply furthers their own career. It rarely seems to be followed by action that could improve our day-to-day working lives (see slide below). The quote comes from the article "*The labour of academia*". The image is a postcard I created for a session on co-creating academic well-being in the CYGNA academic women's network. Inactive complainers are one of my top-3 "challenges of academic well-being".

So, if you are a senior academic reading this, please ask yourself: what *can* I do the change the system? Do you want to stay on the outside, take the moral high ground, remain in opposition, blame everything on "management" and "neoliberalism", and publish a few provocative pieces in top journals. Or are you prepared to get your hands dirty and try to change, or at least tweak, the system by playing a role in shaping and influencing decision-making, whether in formal management roles or informally behind the scenes?

No doubt you will need to make some compromises. No doubt some colleagues will start to see you as "one of the enemies". But ultimately, complaining about how academia is "going to the dogs" is simply preaching to the converted. It might be nice to let of steam, but it doesn't make anyone's life better. So, consider whether you can walk the talk, instead of continuing to sit on the fence.

Digital preservation

Being part of a community means thinking beyond the now, proactively considering the preservation of all elements of the scholarly record (from blog posts to conference papers to tweets and vines), thinking forward to the publics and communities that might find value or interest in our work ten, fifty, or one hundred years from today.

The focus on preservation is a very interesting aspect of being part of a community. As the HuMetrics initiative points out (see above quote), we need to think beyond the here and now. This is something I have thought a lot about in the context of my role as Staff Development Lead at Middlesex University. What would happen if I stepped down from this role? It is what I identified as my third challenge (for the other challenges, see the video on YouTube: "*Supporting Early Career Researchers 2: The Challenges*").

Without sustainability, any structure runs the risk of crumbling when a few key individuals leave. Many of my current initiatives are explicitly directed at ensuring sustainability. First, by creating an institutional memory. At Middlesex, I have done this by circulating monthly research bulletins, and creating a portal on the university's shared drive with access to hundreds of presentations, articles, and videos.

I also recorded videos for key activities I am running, such as my 7-part video series on Publishing in top journals and my 8-part series on Improving your Research Profile, Reputation & Impact. They are available on my YouTube channel. Moreover, I have been running a blog since 2016 with weekly posts on which this book series is based. With the wealth of resources available I have now created a container page (see screenshot below) that collates the most relevant resources in one place.

Working in academia

Container page of resources related to working in academia

Anne-Wil Harzing - Wed 8 Apr 2020 12:40 (updated Fri 29 Jul 2022 14:29)

Working in academia can be challenging, especially as an early career academic. However, there are lots of resources on this website that can help you to navigate your academic job. Here is a list of the most important ones.

After creating an institutional memory, the second element of sustainability is to inspire others to take up leadership positions. This also means being willing to show your own vulnerability. If you seem infallible as a leader, it may be hard to get others to give it a go.

Currently, I am very active in talent spotting, trying to identify who can take over my role when I am no longer available, either alone or in team leadership. Many academics prefer to share leadership roles to have a sounding board and create some redundancy. Partially overlapping tenures in key jobs provide scope for mutual learning.

And finally... a word of caution

Let's ensure that research impact – whether focusing on research outcomes or research processes – is not seen as "yet another tick-box" on a long and constantly growing list of performance indicators.

In today's academic world, it seems we need to be ground-breaking researchers, publishing constantly in the top journals and bringing in bucket loads of research funding, inspiring teachers who are not only entertaining and enlightening their students, but who are also scrupulously fair whilst caring for students' individual differences and providing pastoral care. On top of that many of us need to be effective, efficient, politically astute, and inclusive academic administrator or managers.

Increasingly, we also need to pay attention to our research profile, reputation, and impact, ensuring our work not only has academic impact in the form of citations, but also external impact through external engagement. Whilst I fully agree that all these activities are important in academia, we cannot expect *every* academic to do *all* of these things equally well. Universities need to collectively fulfil all of these functions, but that doesn't mean *every single* academic needs to do all of these, certainly not at *every single* stage of their career.

If we want academics to get serious about research impact, we need to ensure they are *intrinsically* motivated to achieve these outcomes. Most academics truly want to have an impact, they truly want to make a difference both to the scholarly community and in the world outside academia. Many colleagues also want to do their best to support research cultures that are characterised by the values of equity, openness, soundness, collegiality, and community.

However, many universities are still treating funding (input) and publications (throughput) as the "end product" of research. So, we need to dramatically *reduce* performance expectations for funding and publications to allow academics to create real impact, using responsible and inclusive research processes.

Conclusion

This short book provided you with a lay introduction to measuring and improving research impact. Chapter 1 focused on concepts, discussing what research impact is and how it differs by academic role. We also delineated it from related concepts such as research quality and research evaluation.

The next chapter focused on *measuring* research impact. Chapter 2 provided a crash course in data sources and metrics and showed you how to research your citation record with the free Publish or Perish software.

Subsequently, we moved on to *presenting* and *evaluating* research impact. Chapter 3 demonstrated how to make your case for impact, whereas Chapter 4 looked at the role of metrics versus peer review in evaluating research.

The next set of two chapters focused on *improving* your own research impact, discussing the four Cs of getting cited (in an ethical way!) in Chapter 5, and outlining a 7-step process to improve your research impact in Chapter 6.

Chapter 7 concluded the book by emphasising the importance of an impactful research *process*. It discussed the values of the HuMetrics imitative that underlie an impactful research process: equity, openness, collegiality, soundness, and community.

I hope this short guide has helped to demystify the topic of research impact in academia for you, and will provide you with the tools to be successful in creating your own research impact. I would love to hear from you if you feel this book has helped you; feel free to get in touch with me at anne@harzing.com.

Further reading

My blog contains many more posts related to research impact, as well as publishing, and academic careers more generally. Below, I have reproduced a partial list structured by topic. Just Google the title and you will find them easily.

Research impact and funding

The four C's of getting cited
18 Sep 2017 – Anne-Wil Harzing
Short summary of white paper explaining why competence, collaboration, care and communication help to realise the citation impact of your work

Everything you always wanted to know about impact...
02 Jun 2019 – Anne-Wil Harzing
Book chapter providing a quick overview of the what, why, how and where of research impact

Impact is impact is impact? Well, no...
20 Jun 2022 – Anne-Wil Harzing
Reprint of an invited blogpost on the SAGE Social Science Space on disambiguating the concept of impact

Research Academics as Change Makers – Opportunities and Barriers
13 Nov 2021 – Andrea Werner
Reports on a Middlesex University panel discussion on creating external research impact

How to make your case for impact?
13 Jul 2016 – Anne-Wil Harzing
Shows you how to make your case for impact by comparing your papers to the journal average

Making your case for impact if you have few citations
27 Nov 2017 – Anne-Wil Harzing
Provides advice on strategies to demonstrate impact with a very low citation level

How to ensure your paper achieves the impact it deserves?
15 Jan 2018 – Anne-Wil Harzing
Discusses the workflow I use to communicate about a new paper

How to find your next research project?
16 Jun 2016 – Anne-Wil Harzing
Provides suggestions on how to find new and interesting research projects

CYGNA: Working in a Horizon-2020 project
19 Feb 2021 – Anne-Wil Harzing
Reports on our 37th CYGNA meeting dealing with research funding and working in large, funded projects

How to write successful funding applications?
02 Nov 2016 – Anne-Wil Harzing
Provides ten tips for successful funding applications

Finding a Unicorn? Research funding in Business & Management research
05 May 2019 – Anne-Wil Harzing
Explains why university administrators need to be realistic in the amount of research funding they can expect Business School academics to generate

CYGNA: Positionality, team roles, and academic activism
27 Jun 2022 – Anne-Wil Harzing
Reports on our 47th CYGNA meeting, celebrating our 8-year anniversary with our first face-to-face meeting in 2.5 years

Publishing

The four P's of getting published
08 Dec 2016 – Anne-Wil Harzing
Short summary of white paper explaining how performance, practice, participation, and persistence are needed to publish academic papers

The four ailments of academic writing and how to cure them
20 Apr 2020 – Nico Pizzolato
Some golden tips on how to improve your academic writing

How to keep up-to-date with the literature, but avoid information overload?
14 May 2018 – Anne-Wil Harzing
Provides tips on how to keep up-to-date without getting lost

How many references is enough?
30 May 2020 – Anne-Wil Harzing
Some reflections on why more references isn't always better, but how strategic referencing might help

How to avoid a desk-reject in seven steps [1/8]
10 May 2020 – Anne-Wil Harzing
Introduces a 7-step process to increase your chances of getting your paper into the review process

Who do you want to talk to? Targeting journals [2/8]
24 May 2020 – Anne-Wil Harzing
Explains why choosing your target journal is the most important step in the publication process

Your title: the public face of your paper [3/8]
14 Jun 2020 – Anne-Wil Harzing
Illustrates how to create a good title through an iterative process

Writing your abstract: not a last-minute activity [4/8]
28 Jun 2020 – Anne-Wil Harzing
Explains what needs to be included in an effective abstract

Your introduction: first impressions count! [5/8]
11 Sep 2020 – Anne-Wil Harzing
What are the elements of an effective introduction: context, importance, and interest

Conclusions: last impressions count too! [6/8]
18 Sep 2020 – Anne-Wil Harzing
Why conclusions are a crucial part of your paper's key message

What do you cite? Using references strategically [7/8]
03 Oct 2020 – Anne-Wil Harzing
Shows you how references can save you hundreds of words and position your paper

Why do I need to write a letter to the editor? [8/8]
16 Oct 2020 – Anne-Wil Harzing
The last step in the submission process is an important means to "sell" your paper to the journal

From little seed to fully-grown tree: a paper development journey
09 May 2022 – Heejin Kim
A novice publisher providing a "behind the scenes" look at co-authoring for top journals

CYGNA: Writing a literature review paper: whether, what, and when?
19 Sep 2021 – Anne-Wil Harzing
Reports on our 41st CYGNA meeting on the challenge of publishing literature review papers

Want to publish a literature review? Think of it as an empirical paper
23 Apr 2021 – Tatiana Andreeva
What to consider if you want to publish a literature review paper

CYGNA: The wonderful world of book publishing
12 Dec 2020 – Anne-Wil Harzing
Reports on our 35th CYGNA meeting with three publishers discussing textbooks, research books and practice books

---

Own your place in the world by writing a book
11 Dec 2018 – Nico Pizzolato
A passionate plea to consider publishing a book at least once in
your academic career

IB Frontline interview: mentoring section
03 Jan 2022 – Anne-Wil Harzing
Introduces the third section of my IB Frontline interview about my
role as a mentor and my top tips for early career researchers

Career progression

CYGNA: Internal versus External promotion
11 Oct 2018 – Anne-Wil Harzing
Reports on our 22nd CYGNA meeting with a presentation giving
tips for internal and external promotion applications

CYGNA: climbing up the academic career ladder
03 May 2021 – Anne-Wil Harzing
Reports on our 39th CYGNA meeting with a focus on career
progression

CYGNA: How do I keep my job (in academia) in uncertain times?
13 Nov 2020 – Anne-Wil Harzing
Reports on our 34th CYGNA meeting discussing jobs losses in
higher education in COVID-19 times

**CYGNA: One size doesn't fit all – Diversity of academic career
paths**
28 Feb 2022 – Anne-Wil Harzing
Reports on our 45th CYGNA meeting in which we discussed four
alternative career paths in academia

Open Syllabus Explorer: evidencing research-based teaching?
15 Nov 2019 – Anne-Wil Harzing
Reviews how the Open Syllabus Project can help academics to
understand their impact on teaching and find the best textbook for
their course

Presenting your case for tenure or promotion?
23 Nov 2016 – Anne-Wil Harzing
Shows how to make your case for tenure or promotion by comparing your record to a relevant peer group

How to create a sustainable academic career
21 Nov 2020 – Anne-Wil Harzing
Reports on Martyna Sliwa's presentation on career progression in the UK higher education environment

How to create a successful academic career: AIB – Ask, Invest & Believe
22 Jun 2019 – Anne-Wil Harzing
Write-up of my contribution to a conference panel on career strategies at the 2017 AIB-UKI meeting in Birmingham

CV of failures
15 Jun 2019 – Anne-Wil Harzing
Explains why rejection and failure are a normal part of an academic career and not something to hide or be embarrassed about

Publish or Perish increases transparency in academic appointments
14 Oct 2016 – Anne-Wil Harzing
Illustrates how PoP has been used to expose nepotism and incompetence

CYGNA: Careers, mobility and belonging: foreign women academics in the UK
02 Jun 2018 – Anne-Wil Harzing
Reports on our 15th CYGNA meeting with a special emphasis on the challenges for female foreign academics in the UK

Why are there so few female Economics professors?
11 Nov 2018 – Anne-Wil Harzing
Short summary of my article in Economisch Statistische Berichten on gender bias and meritocracy in academia

We need a different kind of superhero: improving gender diversity in academia
12 Jan 2021 – Jill A. Gould
Collects the resources developed for the 2020 AoM symposium on creating gender inclusive academic environments

WAIB Panel: Academic career strategies for women in the UK
01 May 2018 – Anne-Wil Harzing
Reports on a WAIB Panel at the AIB-UKI meeting in Birmingham April 2018

Social media

Social Media in Academia (1): Introduction
16 Jan 2020 – Anne-Wil Harzing
An introduction into my 8-part blogpost series on social media

Social Media in Academia (2): Comparing the options
28 Jan 2020 – Anne-Wil Harzing
General recommendations on how to use social media professionally

Social Media in Academia (3): Google Scholar Profiles
10 Feb 2020 – Anne-Wil Harzing
Provides recommendations on how to get the best out of Google Scholar Profiles

Social Media in Academia (4): LinkedIn
27 Feb 2020 – Anne-Wil Harzing
Provides recommendations on how to get the best out of LinkedIn

Social media in Academia (5): ResearchGate
09 Mar 2020 – Anne-Wil Harzing
Provides recommendations on how to get the most out of ResearchGate

Social Media in Academia (6): Twitter
27 Mar 2020 – Anne-Wil Harzing
Provides recommendations on how to get the best out of Twitter

Social media in Academia (7): Blogging
13 Apr 2020 – Anne-Wil Harzing
Provides recommendations on how to start with blogging

Social Media in Academia (8): Putting it all together
27 Apr 2020 – Anne-Wil Harzing
Final posting in the social media series explains how different social media can reinforce each other

Social Media in Academia: Using LinkedIn to promote your research
08 Apr 2021 – Christa Sathish
Tips and tricks for using LinkedIn to promote your research

How to digitally market yourself: a beginner's guide for students and academics
06 Nov 2021 – Christa Sathish
Handy tips and tricks to start building a digital presence

Other academic skills

Be proactive, resilient & realistic!
07 Jan 2020 – Anne-Wil Harzing
Argues that as an academic you are an independent professional shaping your own career

How to prevent burn-out? About staying sane in academia
12 May 2016 – Anne-Wil Harzing
Provides twelve suggestions on how to prevent burn-out and keep your sanity

CYGNA: Work intensification, well-being and career advancement
08 Dec 2019 – Anne-Wil Harzing
Reports on our 29th CYGNA meeting dealing with workloads and work intensification

On academic life: collaborations and active engagement
19 Jun 2018 – Anne-Wil Harzing
Discusses Martyna Sliwa's articles on the different rationalities underlying research collaborations and the need to get involved in managing and shaping the university organisations we work for

Want to impress at an academic job interview?
24 Jan 2017 – Anne-Wil Harzing
Shows you how to use PoP do some intelligence gathering to make a good impression at a job interview

CYGNA: Working effectively with support staff in academia
06 Mar 2018 – Anne-Wil Harzing
Reports on our 18th CYGNA meeting with a presentation on working with support staff and a discussion of boundaryless careers

CYGNA: Life-long learning in academia
03 Apr 2019 – Anne-Wil Harzing
Reports on our 25th CYGNA meeting with presentations on an Erasmus visit and participation in the Aurora program

How to hold on to your sanity in academia
11 Apr 2019 – Steffi Siegert
Steffi Siegert's powerful contribution that sums up everything that women can be facing in academia

CYGNA: Negotiation workshop
15 Feb 2020 – Anne-Wil Harzing
Reports on our 30th CYGNA meeting dealing with negotiation styles

How to promote your research achievements without being obnoxious?
01 Dec 2018 – Anne-Wil Harzing
Provides some quick and easy to implement tips on how to promote your academic work

CYGNA: Resistance to gender equality in academia
15 Mar 2021 – Anne-Wil Harzing
Reports on our 38th CYGNA meeting dealing with one of the ultimate gender topics

What is that conference networking thing all about?
01 Nov 2017 – Anne-Wil Harzing
Reflections on the importance of networking in academia and tips on how to do it

CYGNA: Supervising and being supervised
02 May 2022 – Anne-Wil Harzing
Reports on our 46th CYGNA meeting where we discussed our experiences of PhD supervision, both from a student and from a supervisor perspective

Meeting an official guest or your academic hero?
15 Sep 2016 – Anne-Wil Harzing
Shows you how to prepare for any academic meeting in 5-10 minutes

www.ingramcontent.com/pod-product-compliance
Lightning Source LLC
Chambersburg PA
CBHW070812050426
42452CB00011B/2003

Books in the series "Crafting your career in academia":

- Writing effective promotion applications (August 2022)
- Publishing in academic journals (November 2022)
- Creating social media profiles (February 2023)
- Measuring and improving research impact (May 2023)
- Using the Publish or Perish software (August 2023)